# MASTERSTROKE

# MASTERSTROKE

## Use the power of your mind to improve your golf

WITH

# NLP

NEURO LINGUISTIC PROGRAMMING

# Harry Alder
# and Karl Morris

PIATKUS

First published in hardback in 1996 by
Judy Piatkus (Publishers) Ltd
5 Windmill Street, London W1P 1HF

First paperback edition 1997

*A catalogue record for this book is
available from the British Library*

ISBN 0 7499 1651 6 (hb)

ISBN 0 7499 1715 6 (pb)

Edited by Carol Franklin
Designed by Chris Warner
Illustrations in Chapter 5 by Mick Stubbs
Cartoons by Ron McTrusty
Diagrams by Chartwell Illustrators

Typeset by Professional Data Bureau, London SW17
Printed and bound in Great Britain by
Biddles Ltd, Guildford and King's Lynn

## Dedication

In memory of Gwynne Morris, who made all this possible, and to Margaret Morris, who continues to support me.

# CONTENTS

# FOREWORD
## by Ian Woosnam MBE

When I told the assembled golf press at the Collingtree British Masters last year that I was reading one of Harry Alder's books on Neuro Linguistic Programming, there was general surprise. This was for a couple of reasons. First, they found it astonishing that I had used some words that had sent them searching for their dictionaries; and second, because I think the press, along with most other people (including, I admit, myself), had always thought of me as a golfer who used the 'natural' physical skills I was lucky enough to have been born with, and didn't have to spend much time on the 'mental' side of the game.

For some time I had been concerned about the difficulty I was having rediscovering the form that had taken me to the US Masters title and the World No 1 ranking in 1991. My poor form on the course had extended to my losing belief in my ball-striking ability, which had always been the basis of my game. In short, I had lost confidence in my own ability to hit the shot which I wanted to hit at a given moment.

What I have learnt from Harry's books on NLP and from several discussions with Harry since then has reminded me of the techniques, the thought processes and the state of mind that I enjoyed in my best years and which I feel I am rediscovering now - the ability to visualise shots before striking the ball, to remember, in an almost physical way, successful shots which I had hit in the past, to recreate 'swing feelings' and to blank out those unhelpful negative feelings. I call on these 'mental' strengths almost uncon-sciously. Already I am seeing the benefits in my improved form and tournament wins in 1996.

The time that I have spent with Harry and Karl has opened my eyes to the importance of the right mental approach. Golf is not just about hitting a shot and building a good score; it depends on practice and preparation. You may think that golf is a physical game, and that natural ability and physical practice are the fundamental factors that shape your game. I now know that this is not the whole story. I guarantee that reading *Masterstroke* will open your eyes, not only to techniques you would never have thought of using to improve your game, but also to the enormous importance of the correct mental attitude and preparation.

I recommend you read *Masterstroke*. NLP helped my game. It will help yours too.

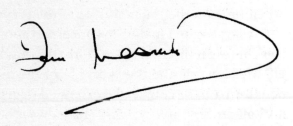

# PREFACE

This book is the result of a unique partnership - a golfer and an NLP practitioner and writer.

Karl Morris is the PGA professional and a full-time golf instructor at Douglas Valley Golf Academy in Bolton, Lancashire. For a long time he has been convinced of the importance of the mental aspects of the game of golf, and of a widening gap in this side of teaching and play. In particular, he was concerned about a massive emphasis on the technical, analytical side of the game, and especially the swing, while there remained ignorance about the part the *mind* plays. Otherwise talented club players could not cope with the slightest pressure situations, and seemed to be at the mercy of temperament and attitude. Unpredictability and inconsistency blocked real improvement, and the fun for many seemed to be no longer there.

The breakthrough came when Karl started to study and apply the principles of neuro-linguistic programming (NLP), which was already bringing outstanding results elsewhere in sport, as well as business, education and self-development.

Harry Alder, a businessman and non-golfer, has worked for many years with business managers. He has met a similar bias toward analysis, at the expense of intuition, imagination and the skills that real leaders need to cope with business demands and constant change. His research has covered the extraordinary success of NLP in sport as well as business, and he has quickly established himself as a popular international writer on the subject. His book

*Think Like a Leader* (Piatkus), involving first-hand contact with more than 150 top business leaders, confirmed the importance of a 'right brain' approach in personal excellence in any field of activity. The impact of several successful books by Dr Alder, including *NLP: The new art and science of getting what you want* (Piatkus) reached well outside business and management circles, and attracted the attention of 'thinking' sportspeople including golfers. This led to the important first meeting between the co-authors that resulted in *Masterstroke*.

There is no shortage of golf books covering the technical or physical aspects of the game. In a few, mental topics only are addressed and readers (in some cases already confused) are presented with an either/or situation. In reality, the mind and body cannot be considered separately, and a completely new approach is needed if golf is to experience quantum improvements on the scale that NLP has brought about in other fields, including other sports.

Our solution is to combine state of the art understanding about the mind from developments in neurology and psychology, including NLP, with the physical and technical aspects of the game with which golfers are so familiar.

Whatever the uniqueness of golf, so many aspects of it are common to other sports and indeed to life generally - the need for confidence and a positive attitude, the ability to handle pressure, the skill to focus on the immediate job in hand and so on. The refreshing and sometimes provocative non-golf perspective that Harry Alder brings offers insights that many club players and professionals, occupied as they are with swing analysis, would rarely encounter. As a PGA professional, Karl Morris has ensured that the real needs and problems of golfers are fully addressed, and that the reader is comfortable with familiar jargon and pertinent illustrations. Karl has also identified the main questions that golfers ask, and these are tackled head on from a unique mental perspective, drawing on the NLP expertise and wide self-development training experience of Harry Alder.

As well as being a scholarly and timely contribution to the game, we hope this book offers you extraordinarily effective ways to improve your scores and lower your handicap. Read *Masterstroke* with an open mind and be ready to experience some fundamental changes. We promise you that you will quickly get much more pleasure out of the game of golf.

Finally, we are grateful to Ian Woosnam for his valuable time and cooperation in making *Masterstroke* possible.

Harry Alder and Karl Morris
September 1996

# 1 ▷ BREAKING THROUGH THE MIND BARRIER

*THERE ARE* a number of specific ways to dramatically improve your golf scores and reduce your handicap. Here are some examples: 1. Don't let your last shot affect your present one.  2. Focus on the target you want to hit rather than on the hazards you want to miss. 3. Don't think about your swing mechanics while you are playing. That's just a start.

What about the ability to be calm and confident whenever you want to be? Or being able to relax under pressure? Or transferring your skill in practice to a real game?  These are all well-known mental aspects of the game which can be readily overcome once you know how. They are mental skills or strategies that can be learnt. Any one of them is worth perhaps half a dozen strokes a round - perhaps more if you easily get emotional, have difficulty concentrating or are self-critical. And we shall meet others as we go on.

Together, these skills account for the difference between a player of abject mediocrity and an Open champion.

Quite simply, this is what the game of golf is all about. Imagine being able to stay focused, remain calm and confident, and consistently perform to your full potential. These are just some of the benefits of the mental control techniques you will learn from this book. The bottom line is better scores and a lower handicap.

Recent developments in applied psychology such as neuro-linguistic programming (NLP) now enable you to take control of these mental aspects of your game with outstanding results in terms of scores, handicap - and the pleasure you get. A few simple but profound principles have been translated into techniques that anyone can use. There's not much theory to digest, because NLP is all about what *works*. It shows you *how* rather than necessarily *why*. Nor is any great leap of faith required, other than accepting the fact that you can think whatever you want to think, which is what mental control is all about. This book will give you the know-how. After all, each of the common 'problems' above has already been successfully overcome, or *no one* would be shooting low sixties scores, achieving par with any consistency - and earning millions of pounds into the bargain. So we don't have to reinvent the wheel. NLP models the way outstanding performers act and think, in a way that you can use to bring about similar outstanding results. It's a matter of:

○ finding somebody who does well what you want to do;

○ spotting 'the difference that makes the difference'; and

○ using their 'success strategy' to do yourself what they can do.

This is the essence of human modelling, the technology of

which has grown dramatically in recent years. It has revolutionised learning and achievement in all sorts of areas and is now producing remarkable results in golf. The great Bobby Jones learnt golf by imitation, and kept his mimicking skill all the way through his career, so you will be in good company as you learn these skills for yourself. But modelling is just one example of how our increasing knowledge of the mind can be applied to behaviour, and you will learn how to use your mind to improve every part of your golf.

Successful examples can be found at all levels of golfing ability. For instance, Graeme, in his late fifties and recently retired due to ill health, decided to take up golf as a form of relaxation, never having held a golf club in his life. After half a dozen lessons, and using the modelling techniques we will describe in this book, his first ever venture on to a golf course produced a score of 93! As experienced readers will know, many younger golfers take two or more years to break 100. Into the bargain, Graeme is finding the relaxation and pleasure that were his main reason for taking up the game.

Laura is a very different story. She had played for several years but was frustratingly stuck at a maximum handicap of 28 - which actually overstated her true ability. In her case, after relearning some fundamentals, she concentrated on simple visualisation techniques to get into a positive state before each shot. In one year her handicap fell to 14.

These are ordinary players, rather than exceptional young high flyers. Higher up the skill range, world greats from Hogan to Player and Price to Woosnam, and many more, have depended on the mental techniques you will learn here, and attributed these, rather than technical perfection, to their outstanding success. The methods often seem almost miraculous, yet have been successfully used at every level in the game. And they don't take for ever. Although, as in the case of Graeme and Laura, any worthwhile improvement happens over a period, there is actual change immediately, so success breeds more success. And the learning process is itself enjoyable, which is a welcome bonus. In this book you will learn important principles that will immediately make sense, and simple techniques you can use straightaway to make big inroads into your scores.

# A Mental Game

Most golfers admit that the game is largely a mental one. Some talk of it being 90 per cent or more in the mind, especially at critical shots in an important game. But golfers, including professionals, nevertheless spend most of their time and effort on the physical or mechanical aspects of the game, and in particular the swing. Modern method teachers say there is only one way to swing a club, and single-mindedly pursue mechanical perfection. Few club players practise mental techniques, such as handling pressure, eliminating unwanted thoughts or visualising targets. Most are at the mercy of their feelings, and the more important the shot, the more our body takes on a mind of its own. Consistency is a rare commodity. The mind in golf is largely uncharted territory and, even after successive breakthroughs in our understanding of how the brain works and affects our behaviour, there is plenty of scepticism about, and a reluctance to come to terms with its mystique.

If the game is largely mental, and average golfers spend a tiny fraction of their time and attention on it, something is very wrong. And to harness the more or less unlimited potential of your mind big changes might be needed, in the way you think as well as in what you do. So it is important to take it one step at a time, and in this chapter we will put the mental game into perspective before introducing you to the principles and techniques that will change your game for life. We will also introduce the four-step Masterstroke model which will be the basis of all your learning and improvement.

Here are some of the questions that golfers ask repeatedly before opening their minds to the Masterstroke methods we will describe. We will deal with these first so that you will get maximum benefit from the rest of the book.

○ Where does new technology and improved equipment fit in with a mental approach? Isn't that where we should concentrate?

○ How important is the swing, and how can thinking affect it?

○ Isn't this just positive thinking or the Inner Game?

○ Is this for anybody or just certain kinds of personality?

○ Isn't it just a matter of trying harder and doing your best?

○ Where does the *unconscious* mind come into it?

○ Can I depend on my brain if the rest of my body lets me down so often?

○ Can professionals benefit from the methods or, for that matter, novices?

## *Mind-boggling technology*

If mental processes are so important in golf, where do all the technological improvements in equipment and coaching

methods fit in? As with all sports, the paraphernalia of golf
has got better over the years. Clubs, heads, shafts and grips
have improved out of all recognition in line with the mind-
boggling technology around us. We have computer analysis
and video to make possible state-of-the-art tuition. Course
design and green care is better than ever, and by and large
our 'tools' are the best that money can buy.   Lee Janzen,
however, says:

> To me, the biggest change in golf is not the ball or the
> shafts, it's in the mind. Golfers are better because they
> think they are. They do not stand on the tee and think
> 'Oh, my God, that's Jack Nicklaus.' They think 'That's
> Jack Nicklaus and I'm going to beat him.' It's like the
> four minute mile. Roger Bannister did it and 32 people
> did it the same year. Three hundred did it the next.
> Why did all those people suddenly get faster? Because
> they believed they could be.

Janzen has pinpointed the important confidence factor in
those that make it to the top, and also the psychological
barrier that Bannister faced but which is common to every
sport including golf.   But for most golfers, the reality of
results does not stack up with all of the technology. Overall,
scores refuse uncannily to budge from the level of years ago,
defying all the leaps of science and technology which seem
to have affected other sports.

## Why are scores not getting lower?
The opening address of the 1994 USPGA teaching summit
held in San Francisco entitled 'Why are scores not getting
any lower?' addressed this dilemma. Of course there are
opposing factors involved, not least ever-lengthening

courses, which can probably be matched by ball design. But still the 'problem' is felt acutely at every level in the game, and not least by professional players and coaches. Alarming inconsistency and freak, unaccountable shot-making causes untold frustration to countless hard-trying amateur enthusiasts. With the best of tools, many seem to go backwards, despite conscientious practice and openness to criticism. The average club golfer's handicap languishes in the twenties and many - even with present methods of coaching and self-development - will not break the hundred barrier. Many are stuck in a frustrating zone of unremarkable competence - of mediocrity. Most excel only in their *inconsistency* from shot to shot and game to game. From time to time their handicap drops a couple of strokes, only to creep back again, as self-esteem falls and the old enjoyment of the game gets increasingly rare.

Top professionals suffer the same heartaches, and the magazines are awash with stories of roller coaster careers. For many, amateurs and professionals, the fun, or even the basic pleasure goes out of the game. But with a little thought the root cause of the paradox posed by the 'San Francisco question' is obvious to amateurs and professionals alike - it is not so much to do with method as *mind*. It is not so much to do with ballistics as *belief*.

So we have some catching up to do in the mental aspects of the game. But at least we have identified where the problem lies - it's a matter of grey matter. If the game is 90 per cent in the mind and played between the ears it becomes a bigger factor the closer you get to scratch. It doesn't go away. The good news is that we now have the technology to harness our personal goal-achieving resource and apply it to the most challenging of games.

## Ballistics or belief

So much for technology. What about the all-important swing? How does it relate, for instance, to our self-belief or the state of mind we happen to be in? David Leadbetter's quote about Ian Baker-Finch says a lot:

> He tells me that when he stands up there he has a mental image of disaster. Half-way down the swing a picture comes into his mind that he'll either hit it out of bounds or even miss it altogether.

And that was said four short years after Ian's Open victory at Birkdale (later references to the 'Open', if golfing purists will forgive me, will be to the British Open). What is the value of a perfect swing and endless hours of practice if 'pictures in the mind' can kill off Open champions?

Short of breaking a leg, nothing could stop Henry Cotton from winning the British Open at Royal St George's, Sandwich, but his nervous stomach very nearly did it. He arrived on the first tee too early and sat for 15 minutes alone in the starter's shed. This made him dwell on everything that might go wrong and just how close he was to the title. When he emerged from the shed he was wracked with stomach pains through sheer nerves. The crowd watched with disbelief as he stumbled through the first nine holes, throwing away his lead. A 10-ft putt later gave him the inspiration he needed to salvage a 79, but it was enough to win the title. As is so often the case, the outcome was little to do with swing mechanics, hours of practice or years of experience. It boiled down to belief and mental control or lack of control.

Dave Thomas came close to winning the British Open

twice in his life. His failure at one was the play-off against Peter Thomson when he pitched the ball painfully short and took three putts. From that moment the pitch shot became a phobia for him and for years afterwards he would rather take a putter than attempt a short shot from around the green. He confessed that his stomach turned whenever he missed a green with an iron because he knew he would be confronted with a pitch shot.

That's what the mind does. The golfing area of the brain is a fragile thing that is terribly susceptible to suggestion.

Contrast those accounts with Ben Hogan's exhilarating mental image of the ball winging its way faultlessly towards the hole, or Gary Player seeing his own name as winner on the scoreboard at the US Open at Bellerive before it came to happen, or Tony Jacklin who, on winning the British Open, said, 'I felt like I was in a cocoon of concentration.'

Or David Graham after winning the US Open in 1981:

I was oblivious to the tremendous pressure I was under. I did not think for a moment of the consequences of a poor shot. There was no fussing over the technical details of my swing. I was almost completely unaware of the thousands of people in the gallery, of the television cameras watching my every move, of the competitors making a run to overtake me. Mentally and physically it was as though I was on automatic pilot. My thoughts were clear, ordered and decisive. All I did was pull a club from the bag, swing, and the type of shot I envisaged would come off perfectly.

Greg Norman's historical collapse in the closing holes of the 1996 US Masters at Augusta, Atlanta, was also a dramatic illustration of what the mind can do. His earlier near wins and familiarity with the course, rather than add confidence, no doubt fuelled self-belief doubts about his vulnerability in the closing holes. As each successive point was lost, Norman's mind must have strayed to where it was its most damaging - back to a harrowing post mortem, and forward to the likely worldwide reaction to such a high profile view of his succumbing once again to competitive pressure. Even his new-found arm waggle was abandoned as he broke the simple rule of sticking to a set up routine in play. Nick Faldo, meanwhile, gave us a lesson in mental focus and self-control.

Whether the way we think helps or hinders, it doesn't just apply to the superstars. Most golfers tend to over-analyse their game - especially the swing. And we are usually too self-critical. The left side of your brain works in this way, but for many activities this can be counter-productive, and a natural, simple swing, for instance, can be ruined. Just because something can be taken apart, like the movement of a grandfather clock, it doesn't mean you can put it together again - at least to the required precision. Now that video recording is widely available, the temptation for radical technical surgery is often too great for the enthusiastic golfer to resist.

But there is a more effective and enjoyable way that operates largely at an unconscious level. We each have an *inbuilt* system for learning and goal-achievement, and this relies a lot on the *right* side of the brain, normally associated with intuition and imagination. This is where much of the mental game happens, and you will learn how to harness this to improve your game.

The average golfer does not improve his or her score stroke by stroke. Improvement usually comes in plateaux.

Typically a score will fall from 95 to 90, or 87 to 81 in a fairly short period. And such learning steps are usually linked to more than a technical or mechanical adjustment. Usually a person's attitude or self-belief changes. There is perhaps a new confidence, better concentration or a more real goal to aim for. Even professionals experience new plateaux - or indeed their game can go unaccountably backwards - again as a result of belief and attitude rather than ballistics or technique.

## Beyond positive thinking and the inner game

Most golf books are about the physical game, and in particular the swing. This is at odds with what most professionals insist: that the game is largely a mental one. But the anomaly goes further. Those books that have identified the importance of the mind are thin on *what to do about it* - specifically.  This book will help you do just that.

○ How do you stop yourself thinking about the bunker you don't want to think about - what do you *do*? The answer is that you think about what you *do* want - your target - and this is explained in the next chapter which is all about setting and achieving goals.  The 'tests for a well-formed outcome' and mental rehearsal techniques could revolutionise your whole approach to the game.

○ How, specifically, do you change a negative self-belief that is ruining your game? Look at Chapter 3, all about beliefs and how to learn to change those that don't help.

○ How many top players have talked of the importance of having confidence? But it is not enough to be told to have confidence if you don't know what to do to get it. Chapter 4 describes how you can 'call up' confidence, or any other state you want, just when you need it.

○ Chapter 5 explains how you can model a perfect swing, without the usual gruelling analysis and self-criticism, and use modelling to improve any part of your game.

○ What does it actually mean to 'practise mentally'? What do you *do*? Chapter 6 on practice explains it all, as well as showing you how you can get more out of physical practice.

○ The final chapter extends the important principles you will learn to the rest of your life, so that your golf becomes a vital learning ground for bigger achievements in your career and personal life. All this goes a long way beyond positive thinking, giving you practical tools you can apply and convert into lower scores and a lower handicap, as well as a new level of achievement in your wider life.

Timothy Gallwey's book *The Inner Game of Golf* identified the importance of the mind in golf, and the different functions of the two sides of the brain. But Gallwey didn't provide the answers to the questions above, or address the other important questions that golfers ask all the time, and which I address throughout this book. Since the publication of Gallwey's and other 'mind' books, whole new fields of knowledge have opened up, and the human brain is at last revealing some of its secrets. NLP establishes a *technology* for modelling the mental strategies that result in success in golf and other sports, and controlling our emotional state and self-beliefs. So the mystique is taken out of human excellence, or mastery. 'If anyone can,' NLP says, 'I can.' *Masterstroke* shows you how *you* can.

## Ordinary people can do extraordinary things

Is this for anybody? 'If anyone can, I can' has a strong anecdotal pedigree. Household name players turn out to be ordinary people, as many golfing autobiographies will confirm. If the super players do seem special, it's because there are so few who went on to learn the *mental* side of the game that produces consistency and handles pressure. We can all take comfort from the fact that it's not all about genetics and a super body. With a fairly average body and a standard issue brain you can *learn* how to play well to just about any level. 'Positive Mental Attitude' rhetoric is turned into practical 'I can' techniques.

Human achievement and excellence is all about using our ordinary resources in an extraordinary way, and golf is a great example. It's ordinary people doing extraordinary things. It's about learning by doing and making mistakes, so creating consistent habits, like Graeme or Laura, or Gary Player or Ian Woosnam. Then it's about *trusting* your mind-body system to come up with the goods. That's what provides the confidence upon which any achievement is based.

Researchers have failed repeatedly to tie this success down to physical build, intelligence quotient (IQ), technical accuracy or the right choice of parents. Instead, it is usually about attitude, temperament, self-belief, 'feel' and an unquenchable desire to achieve. Somewhere in all this there is usually a 'dream' of success. These strong motivators are, however, simply different mental 'strategies' - different, *better* ways of thinking that produce results. Your key resource is your brain, and you are as free to program it to achieve what you want as anybody else.

## Modelling the extraordinary

One of the amazing results of recent discoveries about human thinking and behaviour is that these mental strategies can be *modelled* - learnt and applied by ordinary people. Special modelling exercises are included in Chapter 5 that you can apply both to learning the fundamentals and to improving any aspect of your game.

Levels of achievement previously associated with 'genius' or 'special gift' are now within the reach of all of us. They always were, in fact, but now this human lottery has been replaced by a few reliable principles and methods. Through modelling, upon which much of neuro-linguistic programming was founded, you can now not only master your own mental game but also draw on the 'strategies' of the best players in the world. A Woosnam swing, a Ballesteros recovery shot, a Crenshaw long putt - take your pick! Modelling gives you access to methods that have proved to be more effective than those used by the most expensive coaches and sport psychologists.

## Using your own success memories

But you needn't depend on the experts. The truth is we are all extraordinary and, however rarely, have achieved successes in the past. You have a good collection of *your own* successful brain recordings - those occasions when you too were able to rise above your usual limitations. And those personal successes are empowering mental strategies re-corded indelibly on the hard disk of your memory, to be *used* again and again. You can start to get to know and use your own innate *success memories*, instead of being a slave to innumerable *failure memories*. Each success recording is a valuable asset you can cash in once you know how. It is worth more than the many hours of hard practice in which - let's face it - we acquire far more practice at *failing* than succeeding! That is just in the nature of golf, as in many other areas of life - there are more misses than hits. So modelling uses blueprints of success rather than failure - your own as well as others.

You can also draw on non-golf success memories. You may have far greater confidence, for instance, in some other game or hobby, and you could well use that empowering state of mind in your golf. Your brain doesn't mind - it will do whatever you program it to do. You can therefore model your best in any part of your life and apply it to your golf. For instance you might want to transfer confidence or patience you have in a hobby or other interest to your golf, or be as goal-orientated as you are in your job and career. Conversely, as you gain confidence and self-esteem in your golf, you can transfer them to other parts of your life.

## Trying harder and harder

Not every golfer is ready to accept the changes in attitude and sometimes self-belief that this whole new way of approaching the sport entails. Having read even this far, you are probably not in that category, and hopefully will approach NLP with an open mind. Common sense, as it happens, says that if something isn't working you should try something different. Yet for the most part we tend to do the opposite - we do more or less the same things we have always done. Maybe more efficiently, maybe more technically correct, but basically we do the same things. In other words *we try harder and harder,* without getting better and better - at least in relation to our effort.

In terms of scores, and even the pleasure you are looking to get from golf, it turns out that trying harder doesn't work. Using your mind means being smarter, not just intellectually, but in allowing your mind and body to do what it is well capable of doing without interference. You think fade and the ball fades; you think draw and the ball draws. A simple metaphorical swing thought is not a critical analytical thought. So you may need to *stop* trying - or at least be ready to try something different.

This is hard for perfectionists. And it goes against the grain of the work ethic. Lifelong values like 'try harder', 'be strong' or 'be perfect' may be doing nothing at all for your present-day achievements. It's the 'all or nothing' syndrome. Sometimes you have to stop trying and let go - that's the way many of our mind-body systems work. Look in Chapter 3 at how our beliefs and values can sometimes work in the opposite direction to what we want to achieve, however sensible they seem. Use the 'belief change pattern' to replace them with empowering ones that bring you the results you want. If you are a conscientious tryer, or perfectionist, but aren't getting the results you feel you deserve, a lot of what you learn will be of immediate benefit. Trying harder, practising longer, or analysing in greater and greater detail are not what makes for lower scores and pleasure in the game. Using your mind better makes more sense, and it can be a lot of fun.

## Harness your unconscious mind

The unconscious part of your mind holds the secrets of 'automatic' skills, and that's the part of the brain that doesn't need to 'try'. It is also the home of the intuition and imagination we associate with true champions who make everything look so easy. Each generation marvels at the awesome complexity of the human brain. But although we have hardly begun to answer the big 'whys', we have begun to find out *how* we can use this fantastic resource to achieve real, specific outcomes. So there is no longer any mystery. Answers are there for all of us to see in the way each side of the brain works, and skill habits, like a golf swing, are learnt. The few who achieve excellence do so with apparent ease. They do not depend primarily on *conscious* application of technical knowledge and skill, but a natural, almost child-like, ability takes over. They do it *without thinking*, in any conscious, analytical, trying sense.

Harry Vardon had an instinctive knowledge of his golf muscles, and said he could feel any kind of shot, even though he could not always find words to describe it objectively. Indeed, many golfers speak of 'muscle memory', in which the body accurately follows its subconscious blueprint of success, without the interference of the critical, conscious mind. In fact muscles don't have a memory - it happens in the brain - but we all know what they mean. When you are in the 'flow' or a 'hot streak' it seems so easy. And so it should. This is the way we are designed to work, and this is where excellence lies. Using our fairly standard brainware, we are all capable of achieving it.

You can lay the groundwork for playing at your peak, but then you must let it happen. You can create skills and habits - like 'feel' - by applying the four-part Masterstroke model, described below, which is the 'system' for creating unconscious skills. And the secret is in unconscious, instinctive play. Jack Nicklaus put it like this:

> The golf swing happens far too fast for you to direct your muscles consciously. Frequently I can make minor adjustments in mid-swing, but they are always instinctive, never conscious.

## The power of the mental game

No serious golfer underestimates the power of the mind. Although the mental game goes on unseen, its effects are very real. On the downside a lovely swing can disintegrate, supple limbs on the practice range can become strangely paralysed, and we can be come pathetic slaves to how we feel. Insult is added to injury because we know we can do so much better. It's all in the mind - or maybe 90 per cent of it is. Most golfers play well below their potential, even allowing for other commitments and the time available, and the master key to that potential is in the way we think. But conversely a right mental approach can create confidence and effortless consistency, even with an imperfect swing and second-rate tools.

## The ultimate power source

If so much depends on what goes on in your brain, can you depend on it? Is *every* brain able to achieve what we program it to do? It so happens that our approximately three-and-a-half pound brain hardware is fairly standard. It is certainly not a factor in whether you can rise to the highest levels in sport, however 'mental' the sport is. Even Einstein, so they tell us, used less than 5 per cent of his brain power. The answer lies not in the hardware but in the software. It is in the way you *use* this awesome resource - in the programs you run. And you design and run these programs as you wish, borrowing from others or from successful experiences of your own. Your brain is the control room of your body, and together their potential is extraordinary. So, for all practical purposes, *there is no limit* to what you can do with your mind. The real game is on the inside, and it is all within your control.

## Putting mind power into practice

The opening examples we gave on page 5 of ways of reducing your handicap - concentrating on the shot in hand, aiming for what you want to hit rather than the hazards, and not thinking about the mechanics of your swing - and others we shall describe throughout the book, have two things in common. First, they are to do with how we think - what goes on in the mind. Second, they are, despite the so-called information revolution, little understood by the average golfer.

Even professionals are strangely unaware that we can

influence 'nerves', attitudes and beliefs. This is not surprising, as some of the technology I will refer to is quite new,
and, like any area of knowledge, especially concerning the
human brain, it is hard for the busy person to keep abreast
of what is happening. This doesn't mean that it is heavy
theoretical stuff . In fact, it is quite the contrary. NLP is all
about what works *in practice* - even when we don't fully
understand why. For instance, it can help you to have a
natural, relaxed swing even though you have no inkling of
the hundreds of muscular and chemical activities that
accounted for it. Instead of *analysing* excellence, NLP *copies*
it. It enables you to switch instantly from debilitating fear at
tee off or at a critical putt and become fully controlled,
without necessarily knowing *why* the simple things you did
worked.

Harvey Penick, one of the greatest golfing teachers of all
time and author of the *Little Red Book*, preferred to teach
with 'images and metaphors that plant in the mind the seeds
of shot-making.' This is the right brain way of learning
which plays too small a part in modern coaching techniques.

## Back to basics

Every golfer knows instinctively the issues that most affect
scores - controlling your temperament, focusing, handling
pressure, and so on. In practice, and in response to powerful marketing, we are more inclined towards clever analytical critique about some minute aspect of our swing. Unlike
what goes on in the mind, you can see it, and capture it on
video, even though it may be the last thing you should be
attending to. This does not mean that the fundamentals of
the game, including a consistent repeating swing that hits
the ball solidly, are not important. On the contrary, just like

the habits we acquire when learning to drive a car, the way we learn these basics will dictate the sort of problems we face many years into the game. Learning is about the way we think, and NLP has a lot to say about this. Every part of your game is affected by what goes on in your mind, from the first ball you ever swipe to a deciding putt at the Open. Mental strategies are the foundation of every stroke you make, every score you record. The mental game is not an added extra for professionals, but a basic requirement for every serious golfer.

# Achieve Mastery In Every Part Of Your Game

This book brings together all the knowledge and tools you need to make your mind work for you rather than against you in golf. It describes, in simple language, what you can do about how you think, to dramatically improve your golf. We describe the sort of mental systems that we use to play the game, whether to control physical functions like swinging and putting, or the variety of feelings and attitudes and self-beliefs that dictate whatever we do. Knowing about the processes involved is an important foundation if you are to *trust* these mind-body systems, and so get the best out of them. We also describe specific ways you can make the changes - to control how you feel, to call on a resourceful attitude, even to change long-standing beliefs about your ability that are hindering you from achieving your best. All this will apply to every aspect of the game at every level, from a single putt to winning the monthly medal or turning professional.

The principles and techniques you are about to learn are revolutionising thinking in many areas, not just golf. Other sports, all of which have their own particular mental aspects, are also seeing the benefits, and records continue to be smashed. The outstanding progress in recent years can no longer be explained away by healthier lifestyle, diet and new physical training techniques. These changes have gone on over the years, but there is now a significant new dimension. The *mind* has finally become central to coaching and technique - or to be more precise, the mind-body partnership. Business and education are applying the ideas as well, so that in place of hit-and-miss positive-thinking hype large corporations and other organisations now have effective, predictable ways to get extraordinary results from ordinary people.

Mastery in golf happens between the ears. As we saw, your brain hardware is more or less standard. But by knowing what programs to run and how to run them you can achieve mastery in every part of your game, and convert it into a lower handicap. How much lower? Only your imagination can limit what you are able to achieve, and that, more than anything else, is within your control. As a bonus, you will get a lot more pleasure out of the game, and enter a whole new world of learning and achievement.

## Four-part masterstroke model

The system we have been describing can be expressed as a simple four-part model and applied to your golf as it can to just about any other area of human performance. The four parts are as follows:

1. Decide what you want.

2. Do something.
3. Notice what happens.
4. Be flexible, and ready to change what you do until you get your result.

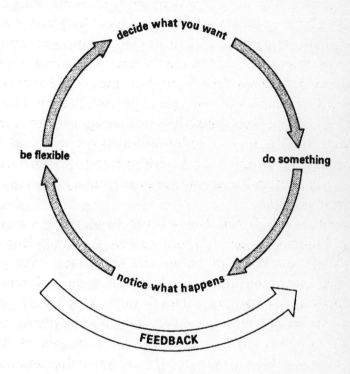

**Figure 1** The Four-part Masterstroke Model

## 1. Decision

Often we don't decide what we want, yet seem surprised when we don't achieve much. The brain needs to have a target towards which it will strive just like a cybernetic goal-achieving system - 'I want to get on to the green.' More often, we decide what we *don't* want - 'I need to keep away from there, miss that, go the left of there, avoid so-and-so.' That is like feeding a missile system with all the targets you want to miss, rather than the one you want to hit - it doesn't make sense. 'Miss' becomes the operative message - the target in the system. And you probably will miss! So whether the goal is unclear, the wrong one, or missing altogether, the effect is disastrous. When you are aware of these mental potholes, you can fix clear, *positive* mental goals that will act for you rather than against you. Chapter 2 tells you how.

## 2. Action

When it comes to longer term ambitions, whether in sport or any other area, many people never get beyond the dreaming or perhaps talking stage. This book, unlike others, does not major on the mind, but rather on the mind-body partnership. You can't separate them. The second stage in the model is *doing something*. Initially, the 'some-thing' may be just hitting out in the right general direction. Then you get better and better each time you *do*.

This is where children can teach us a lot. Because they lack inhibition, they are willing to have a go without worrying about failing or what people think. That's the best way to learn. In golf the tiniest change in what you do can have a big effect on your results. One of the most common tendencies people have when learning to drive a car is overcorrecting the steering, and we tend to make the same mistake in golf or any learning skill. Learn to be sensitive. Don't pull up the roots to see if the tree is growing. If you need an aspirin, you don't have to swallow the whole bottle.

## 3. Acuity

The next part in the cycle is to notice what happens. This brings into play your five senses, and provides the negative feedback that will tell you what you need to do differently.

In due course the ball is struck, and - just like a car driver learning to drive - with repeated practice, it heads in the right general direction. The more you notice what happens, inside and out - and 'sensory acuity' is a skill that can be acquired - the more you will be able to change for the better.

## 4. Flexibility

The flexibility to do something *different* is where many people fall down. We are creatures of habit and get set in our ways, especially in areas of sport and hobbies where we reckon to have some expertise. If you are not hitting the target, it only makes sense to do something if you do something *different*. Do the same thing and you are likely to get the same result. To put it another way, 'If you always do what you always did, you'll always get what you always got.'

## *A dynamic way to learn*

As well as a model for achieving, or getting what you want, this is a learning model. It is the way we learn best. Children and adult 'fast learners' use it all the time. And the whole system is dynamic - you can change any goal, for instance, and start the cycle over again. You can improve a particular stroke or change a troublesome habit. A score that would have delighted you five years ago may no longer motivate you and you now strive for bigger things. But a new goal means doing different things, learning again, exercising perhaps more sensory acuity than you have in the past, and being more flexible rather than set in your ways. And each part of the cycle is crucial - you cannot miss any one stage.

Sensory acuity comes with practice. And a flexible attitude may also take time to develop. But once you understand and trust the process, improvement will come quickly.

Most important, you need to be clear about what you want - decide on your golf and non-golf goals - if you are to harness your inbuilt powers to the full. That is the way we learn to do anything that uses this amazing, inbuilt mastery system. Learning never stops. Doing never stops. 'Failing' or missing, whatever we call it, never stops. It is all part of the trial and error process that creates mental and physical habits that eventually bring success. And you can apply the process to every aspect of your golf and life.

## Failure or feedback

Failure is a concept that does not make sense as far as the masterstroke model is concerned. A child who falls over a thousand times when learning to walk has not failed. As a novice golfer you have not failed if you miss the ball on your first wild swing, or tenth. In each case you learn what happens when you act in a certain way, and go on to try

something different - once, ten times, or a thousand times, until you succeed. Like a missile, each minute correction based on sensitive feedback brings it closer to its target, however small or distant that target. Every so-called failure is an indispensable stepping stone on the road to success.

This principle applies at every level in the game, not just when you are making a stroke. Unless you have the sensory acuity to notice what happens when you do something, and are flexible enough to keep changing until you get what you want, you will continue to practise failure rather than success. The masterstroke cycle applies shot by shot, hole by hole, on the practice round or in competition. It applies to scores and handicaps, and to your longer term ambitions in the game, including the fun and pleasure you want to get out of it. This is a goal-achieving mechanism that can be applied by anybody at any level.

## Starting with the first swing

The mental approach is not just for professionals and low handicappers. It starts with the very first swing, and accounts for maybe 95 per cent of what is happening in the final shots of the Ryder Cup or a major tournament. It is the secret of effective learning - the uninhibited way that children do it. It is about establishing *habits* - behaviours that with repetition are natural and do not require conscious thought, but are nevertheless run from the control room of the brain. Having reached any learning target, which can be a specific kind of shot, playing a competitive game, or any kind or level of outcome, the aim then is consistency. And this is where we need to start trusting the system without interfering at a conscious level.

'If anyone can, I can' is only part of the story. What will

attract erratic, inconsistent golfers are the modelling techniques that prove that 'If I can do it once, I can do it again and again.'

The mental approach applies just as much or more once you have a portfolio of successful golf experiences upon which to draw. For a top professional, large money earnings can hang on a single shot, requiring special concentration and mental control. For the club player, the pressure might come from competition with a particular colleague, or for any of us the association with a particular hole, or type of shot. In each case we need to draw on what we know we can do, and take control of the beliefs and feelings that stop us from doing things in a rational, predictable, enjoyable way. There are enough challenges in golf without the ulcer-inducing agonies we sometimes go through in the name of a so-called *game*. You may have identified with some of the problems and situations I have referred to. These crop up repeatedly and form the specific questions that golfers ask most. But so far they have not had satisfactory answers.

## The Questions Golfers Ask Most

NLP-based principles and techniques can be applied to these very questions, such as:

***Why do I do so well in practice but not on the course?***
Look at Chapter 6, A special kind of practice.

***How can I stop shaking with nerves on the first tee?***
Chapter 6 also gives advice on preparing for important

matches, and Chapter 4 describes techniques for controlling how you feel.

### Why do I play so badly when trying to impress somebody?

You can learn specific ways to maintain focus, Chapter 4. Also when you think about your goals in Chapter 2 you will get your overall purpose into better perspective, and many present concerns and hang-ups will lose their power. You can start to be your own judge - nobody else really cares anyway.

### Why am I so good at other sports but not at golf?

Check out your self-beliefs, Chapter 3. You will find just how irrational some of our self-beliefs are, even though they turn out to be self-fulfilling. Golf is static compared with other games involving a moving ball and requiring hand/eye coordination. So different skills are needed and in particular getting the fundamentals right is vital, which we cover in Chapter 5.

### Why do I feel so unhappy when I finish playing?

What is your personal 'par'? Does enjoyment come only from the score on a card? When you set out to have fun, the chances are you will have some fun. When you have completed your personal 'hierarchy of beliefs' (Chapter 3) you will have this and many other things in perspective.

### How can I improve if I don't have the time to practise?

Have a go at mental practice - Chapter 6. It works a bit like the fast forward on your video, so can be a great time saver, but with great results. The same chapter will also help you with your normal practice sessions.

### Why are my scores so inconsistent?

Because you are affected by whatever is in your mind. Everything you will learn in this book will contribute to your overall consistency.

### Why can't I do as well as I have actually done on past occasions?

You can. Refer back to modelling on yourself earlier in this chapter, and Chapter 5.

### Why do I do better when I don't care about the result?

Because you are likely to be more relaxed, without harmful pressure, and that's the way good golf is played. Look at Chapter 4 - you can actually create that 'don't care' feeling if you want to.

And so on. Important questions such as these, drawn from experience with golfers at different levels, are addressed in this book, spread over the main topics and included at the end of each chapter. The answers in some cases refer you to the parts of the book that address the topics fully. Some of these questions will be the key to your own improvement. And in any event the principles and techniques you will learn will enable you to take control of any aspect of your game, using your mind to the full. Drawing on state-of-the art understanding of how our brains work and using well-proven NLP techniques, this book answers these and many other questions in a simple practical way.

## Summary

In this chapter we have spelled out the importance of the mental side of the game, and the remarkable potential in using modelling and other techniques based on neuro-linguistic programming. We have also laid the foundation of some of the important factors which affect every golfer at every level - the importance of the unconscious mind, the four-part mastery model, the role of 'failure', self-belief, obsession with the swing, confidence, 'over-trying', controlling how you feel, mental practice and so on. In the next chapter we shall look more specifically at goals or outcomes, and in Chapter 3 we will see whether your beliefs are empowering or disempowering in terms of what you want to achieve.

# 2 GO FOR YOUR GOLFING GOALS

*THE FIRST* rule in sport or any form of personal achievement is to decide what you want. Golf is no exception. Science now supports what great achievers throughout history have claimed - human beings are literally engineered for success; we are designed to achieve goals.

Goal-setting was the first stage in the four-part masterstroke model you have just met in Chapter 1. At one level it is quite straightforward. The objective in the case of golf is to get the ball in the hole with the minimum number of strokes. Or you may want to win a tournament. But at the same time you may also wish to impress your boss, keep fit, or perhaps enjoy yourself. So other goals come into play, sometimes important 'life' goals, and one may well affect another. We are not even aware of some of these, but they nevertheless affect everything we do and achieve.

Some goals are more like dreams, and you are drawn towards them over a long period. You don't get to become a scratch golfer, for instance, or win a Masters without starting with a dream. Although top golfers have little in common when it comes to temperament, background or even physical build, they seem to be marked out by a belief in themselves and a dream about what they want to be and accomplish. And these dream-goals existed long before actual success came. They are what fuelled the will-power, discipline, and brute perseverance that are also part of the story of success in any field. So it is worth learning how to set and achieve goals.

When he was a child, Ian Baker-Finch dreamt repeatedly that he was playing in the British Open Championship, and his playing partners were Lee Trevino and Jack Nicklaus. Ian won every time! Byron Nelson, as a young player, dreamt of owning a ranch. Golf, to him was the only way to achieve his goal. So every tournament was 'going for a piece of it'. Asked what was in his mind in the year he won 11 tournaments in a row he referred to his dream. 'That was what I won tournaments for. It's amazing, but once I got that ranch paid for, I pretty much stopped playing. I was all but done as a competitive player.'

The young Ian Woosnam had dreams of becoming a millionaire. Like Byron Nelson, his game also languished when he had no more burning ambitions to go for. Gary Player overcame untold hurdles to achieve his dreams both on and off the golf course. His wider interests outside golf kept him going after many of his contemporaries had gone to grass. Maybe there isn't such a thing as a championship personality, or for that matter an ideal golfer's personality. But a long-term dream, and shorter term goal focus, are all but indispensable.

If you have got something to live for it just seems natural to expend your time and energy on it, or what might eventually bring it about. If you don't, then all the will-power in the world will not keep you going when the going gets tough. So we are back to the mind, and the power of the imagination to set inner goals that turn into reality. Big achievements require big dreams. It's as simple as that. What remains is how to set clear, motivating goals which will have the best chance of success.

## The Power Of A Clear Goal

If you are not naturally 'goal-orientated' you can *learn* how to fix goals in a deliberate way and get the same results as a person who is naturally goal-orientated. Lorraine is a keen golfer who, although getting quickly to a middle level handicap apparently by sheer skill and natural coordina-tion, plateaued out for a couple of years. Only when she went through the discipline of the 'well-formed outcome' you will learn in this chapter did her handicap start to fall again, and continued to do so as her personal goals became bigger and more motivating.

After coming into the game in his late teens Colin reached a handicap of three, overtaking many of his envious club colleagues. One of his secrets is the way he visualises his target shot by shot, and manages to retain the image as part of his set-up routine. He was also very ambitious, so his top to bottom goal focus was unbeatable.

Goals apply at every level, and you will learn how to set your goals within a personal hierarchy so that each one supports the others. This chapter also includes 'right brain' goal setting and you will discover how you can use the same visualisation process Colin used - there is no mystique about it. Top players over the years have used these skills to extraordinary effect. So goals and motivation are not just important at a career or tournament level. You need to be just as committed to a 3-ft putt, and every hole you play. Goal focus is not so much a technique as a way of thinking.

## *Turning wishes into wants*

Not everybody has a burning life-dream as a four year old. Many people don't think much beyond the next weekend. But amazingly, some of the mental technology we now have available can change half-cock wishes into burning ambitions and desires. You can have new dreams just like you can have a new set of clubs. It's all to do with how we think about our goals, and the strategies we use to represent the things we want. 'If Charlie can have a dream, I can have a

dream.' You don't need special DNA or to be super-ambitious. Anyone can harness the power of a clear goal.

It's up to you. If you just want to achieve a little, then a little dream - or a well-defined, realistic goal - is all you need.   But you can be sure that your inbuilt success mechanisms are not the limiting factor. Based on thousands of actual cases, it is statistically very unlikely that your physical build or any genetic feature will be a major factor. Rather, it's the power of your goals that makes the difference. Among sports golf, in particular, is more to do with attitude and outcomes than athleticism. But attitude and outcomes are a feature, not of brain or body hardware, but of brain software. So you can do something about it. You have the free will to think as well as act as you wish.

William James, the most prominent American psychologist of the nineteenth century, when asked to identify the most important finding of half a century's university research into the workings of the mind, replied: 'People by and large become what they think about themselves. What you see yourself becoming forms the inner goal to which you will always be drawn.' You can start to see yourself achieving what you want to achieve in your golf.

## Align all your goals

In fact everyone of us is strongly goal-orientated - it's just that most of what we do is automatic and unconscious. If you are cold you shiver - automatically - to achieve the temperature 'target' that is best for your welfare. If you get too hot you sweat and, just like a car radiator cooling system, you get back to the right temperature target. Nor do you need to think about your breathing - it always operates at the best level. Such targets are built in, or hard-wired. Although requiring negative feedback through the five senses we are all familiar with, they operate *unconsciously*.

Other goals also operate unconsciously. Some people want to impress others, mix in with the crowd, prove their school teacher wrong, or overcome a physical weakness. These might not be as obvious as 'reduce handicap to 10 by next season' or 'win monthly medal', but they have the same powerful effect, and sometimes a bigger effect, than a written down resolution. Because some of our intentions are unconscious, much like an 'accident waiting to happen', we can be pulling in two directions and, not surprisingly, none of our goals is satisfactorily achieved. The 'system' works perfectly - it's just that we unknowingly feed it with the wrong targets. The outcome principles and specific tests you will learn in this chapter will help you to identify all your goals and make sure you are working in one direction.

## Internalising your goals

To start with, you need to simply decide what you want - remember the first step in the masterstroke model? Then you will have to put some order of priority on your goals, if you are to achieve anything worthwhile. But there is more to it. In order to form the inner target of your goal-achieving system, so that all your unconscious powers pull in the same direction, your goal has to be *internalised*. Even at a conscious level, with a perfectly clear overall goal such as a drop in your handicap, you will have to decide what you want stroke by stroke - as interim goals or stepping stones.

But you can do a lot about goals long before you are confronted with a difficult lie of the ball or even face the first tee. And your handicap goal can be a lot more motivating. There are some simple principles involved, and also techniques that involve the use of your imaginative right brain, to properly 'register' your goals.

# The Know-how Of Goal Setting

Having a clear goal is fundamental to success in golf and any other human activity. But for most of us, it doesn't just happen. There is a bit of technology involved. To start with, our goals apply at many levels, from big, long-term life goals to where you want your next shot to land. At one level, for example, you may want to be a scratch golf professional, to have a full and stimulating non-work life, to build up strong relationships, to get fit, or to get away from domestic chores. These big goals are fine, but in practice are often not much more use to your brain than the idea of wanting to be happy or fulfilled. It's like targeting a missile on China or Canada, or wanting a weekend break 'somewhere in Europe'. Many such imprecise goals go unfulfilled for many years, and some - more in the nature of wishes or pipe-dreams - never happen at all. When they do, they are usually supported by more specific, realistic goals at a lower level. In golf these levels may include handicap aspirations, an individual match, a particular round, a specific hole, and of course each stroke. The technology of goal achievement applies at every level. But the techniques, or mental tools, vary.

## Your hierarchy of personal goals

Although the principles of clear goal setting apply in every case, the goals themselves will be of very different *kinds*, as well as levels. For instance an easily measurable handicap goal might be linked with a not-so-measurable desire to have fun, or not to jeopardise your career, family, or other parts of your life. But they are all - or should be - interrelated. A successful shot contributes to a winning hole, then to the round, and so on to your higher handicap goal and other longer term ambitions. But it also contributes to-wards your enjoyment of the game, your sense of self-worth, the recognition you need, and so on. And your goals outside golf - perhaps concerning your family and work, or self-development in other areas of your life - will also have to fit in. So they form a hierarchy, like a family tree, with many lower level short term goals feeding into a handful of bigger, longer term ones. With apologies to John Donne, no goal is an island.

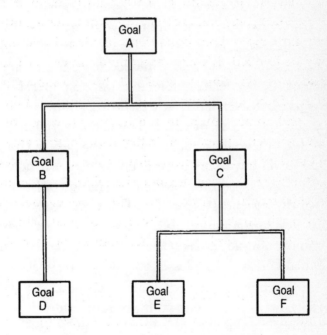

**Figure 2a** Hierarchy of Goals

As Figure 2a shows, your A goal might be to achieve a certain handicap, take part in a certain competition, be-come a professional, or whatever. The next level (B and C in the diagram) might be to do with your scores over the next year or six months, your overall time commitment, or some major part of your game. High level non-golf goals may also come here, perhaps to do with your career and relationship. Depending on how important golf is in your life, it may not figure at the top level at all.

The sort of goals to include at the next level (D,E,F) might include resolutions about your weekly practice, your score for a specific course or hole, and non-golf goals to do with your family, finances, job qualifications or hobbies. In the 'tree', these will contribute to one or other of the higher level goals. If you've never related these to each other now is a good time, as you can be sure that your success - in golf as in other areas of your life - will be affected by other goals.

That's probably as far as you need to go in putting your outcomes (goals, desires, objectives) on to paper, but note that every goal, even if not written down, should contribute to a higher level goal, or you will have no overall direction. Every shot outcome - what happens in the next ten minutes, perhaps - will form part of your bigger score, handicap, or enjoyment goals. Gain a string of successful outcomes at stroke level, and your course score and handicap goals will soon follow. Your top golfing goal (say a handicap target) may have one or more non-golf goals at the same level, and these in turn will depend on achieving lesser but supporting goals.

Once you have fixed clear goals, such as scores, you will soon sort out how to spend your time and effort. If a certain kind of practice has more effect on your scores than re-analysing your swing, your decision will be easy. What you learn about the mental side of the game will help you to get the right perspective. So it's lower level, including stroke by stroke, goal focus that makes all the difference - provided these support your higher level goals. A dream has to be turned into reality, and *every shot counts*.

At the other extreme you can go to a higher level which usually goes beyond golf and concerns your health, important relationships, quality of life, and more spiritual outcomes (why do I want a lower golf handicap?). Somewhere at the top there is usually happiness, fulfilment and contentment. So where these are missing from your game - some speak of the fun and pleasure being long since lost - the chances are you will not advance far, as your direction, wherever it is taking you, is not helping your bigger, important outcomes. The same will apply when there is conflict between your golf and non-golf goals. Something may have to give, and more often than not you lose out on both counts. Aim for what it termed *outcome congruence*. It's like a football team acting as one, but in this case the players are the different outcomes of 'parts' of you in your mind. Working together they are a formidable team.

## *Sorting out your golfing goals*

What type of goals do you set for yourself? Some might concern your *knowledge* of the game, others what you *do*, others what you *are* or how you see yourself ('I want to be...'). Some might involve the physical or material trappings of success, and other desires will be more to do with relationships. Your personal hierarchy will probably have longer term goals at the top (such as to become a professional, or play off a certain handicap) and more immediate ones (such as a practice or game objective this weekend). Most 'goals', such as a desire to finish up just to the right of the cedar tree, hardly get a thought, even though all your bigger goals depend on them. However spontaneous or insignificant they seem, most of the principles and some of the techniques you will learn can be applied to them. Repeated success at a shot level is what eventually will win the Open.

## *Making a start*

Make a start by listing all the things you want to achieve - to have, know, be, do, etc. - both inside and outside golf. Use Figure 2a on page 43 as an illustration, but make this your unique list of desires, wishes, and goals. This will form the higher end of your hierarchy of outcomes. Your outcomes - what you decide you want - will affect your motivation and in turn what you do, your actual performance, and of course the results you achieve, so it's worth doing it seriously. You may find it helpful to use a checklist so that you cover all the kinds of outcomes we typically aspire to. Here are some questions that will provide a checklist:

○ What do I want to *know*?

○ What do I want to *do*?

○ What do I want to *have* or *get*?

○ What do I want to *be*?

○ What do I want in terms of *relationships*?

Before reading on, scribble down some answers now. These categories have special significance, and are based on an NLP model know as Life Content. The different ways we approach our goals are examples of meta programs, or high level thinking and behaviour strategies. They reflect different preferences in individuals, including in the way we are motivated. Answer the questions first in respect of your golf, but then address also other parts of your life. These outcomes need not be 'shot specific' or 'game specific' such as a tee off on the seventeenth next weekend. But they can concern certain kinds of shot, for example long putts or bunker shots, as well as goals you want to achieve in the coming weeks and months. So your list will stay valid for a while.

## Knowing

Some people are very concerned about *knowing*. They need to understand all the theory, know the rule book inside out, be knowledgeable about golf generally, as well as their own strengths and weaknesses, and the technicalities of their every stroke. This will apply to a lot more than golf in their lives, such as absorbing all the information they can find before making a car, hi-fi, or other purchase. If this is not you, you probably know somebody who is like this.

## Doing

Others want to actually accomplish things, are usually ready to have a go at anything new, and get pleasure in the action. That is the *doing* category. Such a person only consults the instruction manual when things go wrong - if even then. They want to get on and *play* rather than spend time learning the fundamentals off the golf course.

## Getting or having

Others are acquisitive, and want to *get* or *have*, and their various goals reflect this. As well as fancy clubs and equipment, this desire is also met by certificates, trophies and other tangible evidence of achievement.

## Being

Then again, a person who wants to *be* something - to *be* a scratch golfer, to *be* consistent, to *be* in control of their temperament, to *be* a match winner, to *be* admired or respected - thinks about their goals in that particular way.

## Relating

The final *relating* category is often present in the previous
ones - a person might do something to make somebody
happy, or get knowledge in order to gain respect or ap-
plause. In some cases it is an overriding factor in goal
setting. The important thing is to recognise how you set
your goals, and what drives you to succeed.

How you *express* these goals ('I want to *be* a scratch player,'
'I want to *do* something about getting down to scratch,' 'I
want to *know* where I'm going wrong with bunker shots')
often indicates your preference, although you may not
otherwise be aware of it. So it helps to state your goals,
initially at least, spontaneously and quickly. Although you
probably have a preference for the way you think about your
outcomes, no doubt all the categories will apply in different
situations and to some level, so they do form a useful
checklist.

## *Getting your goals into order*

Having made out your list, the next job is to get them in
some order. Usually small, shorter term goals act as stepping
stones towards bigger, longer term ones. For example, you
might need to increase your knowledge in a certain area
*before* you can do want you want, and in turn be what you
want to be or achieve the relationship goal you are after. Or
you might want to have a go at something before you get to
understand what is happening. In this case *doing* comes
before *knowing*. Just as in making a cake, the order in which
you mix the ingredients can mean the difference between
success and failure. Trophies and material evidence of
success are important for some people, and in the professional

game this takes the form of actual money rewards. This is the *having* or *getting* category, which, in terms of interim goals at least, may also involve getting the right set of clubs, or other material paraphernalia you think will solve your problems. People who strongly prefer to think in terms of getting and having may have to build in material rewards to keep them motivated - an evening meal out, new compact disc, or other treat for achieving a practice result, or for achieving a planned weekend score. Getting an order of priority on your goals will help you to ration your time and effort, for instance in practising, but it will also help to achieve harmony with non-golf goals.

The importance of this exercise is first as a checklist to help you to think of as many personal goals as possible, so that you can apply some tests to them shortly, to make them more 'robust' and achievable. Secondly, it will help you understand your particular preference (knowing, getting, doing etc.), and the relative importance of different kinds of goals to you. You may well recognise the goal categories more easily in others than yourself. But knowing yourself is the first step in mastering anything. As you instinctively write down your goals, the words you use will tend to show the category, just as in the examples we used earlier.

## *Getting your goals in harmony*

Next you have to make your goals compatible, or congruent, and this might also affect their ranking. After listing in approximate order of importance, ask the question: 'If I could just have one of these, which would I choose?' or, if you like, 'If I had to forfeit one of these, which would it be?' A goal to spend a lot more time with your family, for instance, might not reconcile with an ambitious goal to get your golf handicap down. Similarly, your career or professional training goals might also have to compete with your time and resources. Sometimes real conflicts will become apparent. Rather than simply adjusting the ranking, you may have to amend the goals themselves, or eliminate some altogether. Usually time and money and other interests are in competition. Don't kid yourself that you can confine your golf to a watertight compartment and exclude the rest of your life. Even top professionals - or at least those that stay at the top - have balancing outside interests. Your brain is unlikely to accept artificial goal compartments and sooner or later there will be confusion as to which target is the one to go for, and you are likely to lose out all round. It is better to sort out the competing demands in your life before you embark seriously on anything, rather than in the middle of it, by which time it is usually too late to clear up the mess.

There still remain all the lower level golf goals, at match, round, hole or stroke level that you set (consciously or unconsciously), and follow day by day and moment by moment. These, by their nature, will tend to change more than life type goals, to fit a particular strategy, playing partner, the weather, the actual lie of the ball, or whatever. There are nevertheless some useful principles and tests you can apply to these as well as the goals on your list. Every outcome can be 'well formed'.

Thousands of conscientious golfers are stuck at a high to middle handicap level because they have not really sorted out their goals in golf or life. From the following exercise you will finish up with a single hierarchy of goals, that mixes golf and non-golf outcomes. This will show how one goal depends on another - hence their order of priority or ranking in the hierarchy - and will also indicate what has to be changed, or even abandoned. You will then be left with a more congruent set of goals that will give you a far better chance of success.

## Exercise: Testing Your Goals

These common sense tests for a 'well-formed outcome' have been used successfully in business as well as personal goal achievement, and also in other sports. They will help you to be clear and specific in your personal hierarchy of goals. They apply right down to a stroke by stroke level, so you can use them to see immediate improvement in your golfing performance. So ask yourself the following questions about your goals:

## Is it positive?

Successful golfers have cottoned on to the need to concentrate on where they want the ball to go (a place on the fairway, on the green, or in the hole), rather than where they *don't* want it to go (in the trees, a particular bunker, or at the wrong side of the fairway). When you say to yourself 'Whatever I do I mustn't slice into those trees', what else is happening in your mind? What sort of pictures come to your mind when you think about the rough, the trees, the water, the bunkers? Then what does your mind do with those images? Is it repelled by them, or attracted towards these pretty landscape features? More to the point, what happens to the image of what you really *want* to achieve, but did not get round to thinking about - at least in a realistic *sensory* way? Does what you really want ever register on your unconscious mind as the target you really want to achieve, the 'instruction' your body has to follow? Or are the two parts of your mind - conscious and unconscious - pulling in two different directions - with inevitable consequences?

It is not possible to visualise something that is negative (try *not* thinking about a purple golf ball the size of a tennis ball under your bed; you can't imagine a non-golf ball). What your brain is trying to do is to put a caption to the picture which says 'Please, please don't let me . . .' accompanied by a picture - perhaps with sounds and feelings - of the very thing you don't want. Your brain misses out the caption, sees the picture, and puts it into practice. Then the more you slice, the more you picture it, and so the habit strengthens. Left to its own devices, the 'system' will work perfectly to fulfil its *assumed* outcome. So be positive about the outcome you want.

Apply the rule to non-golf as well as golf outcomes. If your outcome is not to jeopardise your professional exams, or to avoid being away from your children, for instance, ask yourself what would you rather have instead? The new, positive goal then goes on your list. The 'positive' rule is simple: 'Decide what you want rather than what you don't want.'

## Is it specific?

This question will apply more at the lower level of your hierarchy than at the higher level. But even at the highest level, you should apply the test, in order to come up with more specific *supporting* goals. 'To be a better golfer', for instance, is no more use as a goal than 'to be happy'. These are fine sentiments, but don't give your brain much in the way of direction. What, specifically, are the interim or milestone goals that will bring about your bigger desires?

What do you want to do, know, get, etc. that will make you a better golfer? Are your goals to do with your handicap, your health, some part of your game, your enjoyment, the time you spend, the effects on friends and relatives, or what? And is there a timescale to what you want to achieve? Do you want it this week, this year, or before you die? If not, build one in wherever you can to make your outcome more specific.

Harvey Penick tells a story about the young Ben Crenshaw:

> Ben came to me when he was about 8 years old. We cut off a 7-iron for him. I showed him a good grip and we went outside. There was a green about 75 yards away. I asked Ben to tee up the ball and hit it onto the green. He did. Then I said, 'Now, let's go to the green and putt the ball into the hole.' 'If you wanted it in the hole, why didn't you tell me the first time?' little Ben asked.

You decide on your target - the fairway, the green, the hole. But don't underestimate the brain's ability to respond to a specific target.

## Choosing your specific target

The principle applies at every level. What is your goal or target in the case of a bunker shot? Is it the hole, a radius of 3 ft round the hole, a safe part of the green to leave you a reasonable uphill putt, or just 'to get out of the bunker'? Your decision will depend, of course, on your playing level and what you have achieved in the past. But technically, your goal should be *as specific as you can clearly imagine it*. This is just common sense. Would a cruise missile be aimed within a 50-mile radius of its target? Or, in the case of a central heating 'target' would you be content with the room temperature going the odd ten degrees either way? Or what about a tee shot? Is your goal just 'long' or 'straight' or 'on the fairway', or is it more specific? What will the ball actually do when it lands? Where will it come to rest? Or is your goal just to make a technically correct, stylish swing? The choice is yours but you have to choose.

Golf skills need to become automatic, and follow the four-part mastery cycle we met in the first chapter. But feedback can only work when there is a definite target so that you can assess how far off target you are. How specific is specific? The brain sorts out what is reasonable or not - if you simply *cannot imagine* the ball dropping into the hole from where you are, enlarge your target until you can. But try imagining it first, as you may be underestimating what you can do. Remember that if you have done it once you are technically able to do it again and again - it is now to do with the mind. The same principle of what is *imaginable* applies also to winning the Masters, or any other goal. The good news is that the skill of creative visualisation or mental rehearsal, which you can use to reinforce your goals, can be learnt and developed - you will find that later in the chapter. Make a start by making each goal on your list positive and specific.

## Is it measurable?

A specific goal is more likely to be measurable, which is also an important factor in forming an outcome. 'I want to eliminate my hook' might become 'I want to consistently hit four out of every ten long shots to within no more than x yards to the left of my desired target.' That way it's harder to kid yourself, and your brain knows exactly what it has to do. The first goal, as well as being negative, is not on the face of it easily measurable. To start with, what constitutes a hook? Do you measure it in degrees, or yards from the target, or whether it leaves the fairway, and within what 'tolerances'?

Given a little thought, you can come up with your own definitions and measurements, carried out, perhaps, over a period. You thus have a yardstick of success, but one which can be amended as you move progressively towards your ultimate target. You can raise your sights as one success builds on another, but a measurable target is more specific and the brain responds accordingly. The second more specific goal can be measured over a period, and progressively adjusted as you improve. Fortunately, actual scores and handicap are a ready-made measure of success, and you may only have to add a timescale to make your goal specific.

## Quality or quantity?

Measurement may not always be in quantity, but some-times in quality. What if one of your aims is to get fun and enjoyment out of the game? Although you may not be able to measure this in yards, you might well be able to apply a subjective, qualitative measure to whether you achieved what you wanted - for instance on a scale of one to ten. Similarly, when it comes to getting out of the *rough*, there is 'rough' and there is '*rough*', and you are right to feel great when recovering from a shot that on paper is just so many yards from the green, but in practice requires a shot of extraordinary quality. Try, in any event, to apply some sort of criterion of success to the goals you have listed.

If you wish you can vary your goals as between practice and games. A more ambitious measurable target can apply, if you wish, when you are just practising, to reflect the different circumstances, and also to ensure that you are fully motivated when there is no competition or recognition.

You will find much more about practice in Chapter 6.

## Is it achievable?

This is an important test of any goal that concerns its *size*, or perceived size - how big or small it seems to you. If a goal is too ambitious, you tend to mentally blank off, or even panic, and any motivating effect is reversed. Conversely, if a goal is too small it may not motivate us at all. We need to feel a challenge and the rush of adrenalin as we go for what we want. This is a finely balanced judgement. Arnold Palmer was always at his best in adversity and, perhaps, at his weakest when there was no apparent challenge. He was so far ahead of his nearest rival at the Olympic Club in 1966 that his thoughts turned, not to winning, but to whether he could break the course record. In changing his tactics towards the end and going for birdies he did not need, he committed a series of errors which cost him the championship.

The size of the job in hand involves how you perceive the level of challenge, or the degree of difficulty, and how you perceive your capability of achieving the goal. This is illustrated in Figure 2b (see opposite). It involves your 'comfort zone' and personal 'thermostat' beliefs which you will meet in the next chapter. It is different for you, us or Arnold Palmer. Fortunately perceptions are not like bunkers, mountains or brick walls. They can be changed - you can think what you like - so you can operate at the optimal size of goal which is what usually produces excellence and the state of flow we will now discuss.

**Figure 2b** The Flow Zone

## Hot streaks and flow

Top sportspeople talk about being in a state of 'flow', having 'hot streaks', or being 'in the zone'. This is when everything seems to go right, and they operate effectively at this challenging, stretching level. The 'flow' level is different, of course, from person to person, not just in terms of our actual experience and competence in the game, but also in terms of how we respond to risk (including the risk of success), challenges and uncertainty generally. Some people easily get an adrenalin rush, and for others it is a rare event. This also changes with time, and what motivated you a couple of years ago may now seem boring, or what used to make you freeze with anxiety you can now take in your stride. And, as we saw earlier, a goal that is realistic in a practice situation might not apply in a competition, although this gap can be bridged as you start to take control of your mind.

In each of these cases the size of the goal is important for your success. Too ambitious a target - say in bringing down your handicap - can actually turn out to be counterproductive, as you will soon mentally abandon your goal and be left without a realistic one to replace it. You will be lumbered only with a lower self-worth and pessimistic attitude. Armed with your clear goals, and using some of the mental techniques you will learn, the chances are you will lift your sights a long way. You can *learn* the psychological properties associated with 'hot streaks', such as the perceived size of the task, and enjoy many more of them.

## The time dimension

The time dimension is a useful variable to get this aspect of your goals right. Something that might be out of the question in a three-month period might become just possible given a year to achieve it. The trick is to go for the goal that motivates you most. Similarly you can set reasonable targets for a half-hour or one-hour practice session, balancing the time with the degree of achievement so that you stay motivated and stretched. If you set out to achieve a practice goal in half or a third of the time, for instance, it might suddenly take on a new meaning - and even become fun again!

## *What or who else might be affected?*

No goal works in isolation, but within your overall personal outcome hierarchy. This is much like in nature, where even the smallest changes in the environment can have an effect somewhere else, perhaps on a big scale. Sometimes called an ecology check, this is an important factor in all personal goal-setting, just as ecology is in the natural world. The test consists of ensuring that each goal is compatible with the others, both your own and the goals of other people whom you may care about. In the first case you may have to reconcile a personal work or career goal with a golf ambition, and in the second case you may have to reconcile the interests of a partner or your family - somebody else's goals. Although less directly, these outside 'ecological' factors can have a big effect on your achievement.

Sometimes you will identify goals, yours and others', which you have not hitherto been conscious of, and you may need to stimulate this awareness. Ask yourself, of each goal on your list, 'If I achieved this goal fully, what might I lose?' Or 'How would I feel?' Or 'What would then be important to me?' Is there hesitation, doubt, or mixed feelings? Or do you become aware of *different* outcomes you had not thought about, both yours and those of others? If so you may need to rethink the outcomes and interests, or perhaps values and beliefs, that conflict.

The list of goals you are left with, although perhaps shorter and very different to when you started, will now be 'well formed' and your chances of achieving them will be *multiplied*. If you memorise these simple tests and apply them to anything you set out to do it will become a way of thinking, and success will become a habit. You have already learnt some important masterstroke lessons.

## Right Brain Goal Setting

The tests you have applied are logical, commonsense ways to strengthen your goals. Yet there is an even more powerful mental approach to goal-setting and achievement. Your goals are best internalised by clear imagination, or inner representation by pictures, sounds and feelings. An outcome can be clearly 'registered' in a way that even repeated affirmation or 'self-talk' cannot achieve.

Curtis Strange, twice US Open champion, gives an example of this: 'I've always considered my ability to clearly plan and imagine a shot before playing it one of the strongest aspects of my game. I know that the better I do that, the better my chances of pulling off each individual shot.' The technique, known as mental rehearsal or future pacing, has been used successfully at every level in the game, whether in preparation for an important tournament or as part of a pre-shot routine. And it has been proven to be of use in other sports, as well as in business and personal development. In conjunction with more rational, left-brain approaches, as in the tests of a well-formed outcome, it will give you an enormous edge in performance.

## Creative visualisation

When the whole brain, including the right side which can handle images and feelings, is brought into play, the imagined outcome becomes inner reality. To all intents and purposes it is *experienced*. It makes a new or demanding activity seem familiar, just as if it had already happened - which, to the brain, it has. The brain's reality is the real electro-chemical 'firings' that occur whether we experience something outwardly or inwardly. So, by creative visualisation you can perfect a stroke, or any golf skill, or become confident and in a better state of mind to approach the most formidable challenge, or even change a belief, as we shall see in the next chapter. You alter the *structure* of your thinking. A clearly visualised goal then becomes the brain's target towards which all your unconscious powers are directed. So having made the *destination* absolutely clear, the *journey* is left to the 'system' - and much of that happens automatically so you don't have to try. For more about visualisation, see Chapter 4.

A natural, repeating golf swing is a classic example of this automatic system in operation, or of *unconscious competence*, a key ingredient of human achievement in all sorts of fields. The skill is natural and unforced, and economical in effort - exactly the characteristic that is so obvious in top players. It works best when you don't think about it.

Right brain visualisation can work in partnership with the logical decision-making and testing you have learnt about. It is not an either-or matter. When setting your goal priorities, for example, you probably had to do some imagining, or future pacing, to check out whether one goal is more desirable than another. By experiencing *in advance* different goals you can check out whether they fit with your higher level outcomes - such as whether they give the pleasure you thought they would. Most of us know what it is to get enjoyment by anticipating a well-earned holiday, or imagining the car or house we are saving for, so this is a natural and universal thinking skill we have and can use more. Using this technique consciously, however, you can apply your imagination to specific, tested goals, rather than allowing it to dissipate in pipe dreams or wishful thinking. Mental rehearsal is creative; the inner reality you create becomes the target or blueprint for external reality. You are unconsciously directed towards your visualised goal.

## The long and short of mental rehearsal

You can apply mental rehearsal to every shot you make. Although you can never give much thought to the variety of shots you will have to make during a game *at the time* (that's the big mistake), you still need, for every stroke, a clear target. The rules always apply. For most golfers, this is

more of a problem in the long game, as your actual target
is not always in view, and in any event is not in focus as you
address the ball to make your shot. So you will need to focus
perhaps on a tree or some landmark on the horizon. For
putts, especially short ones, you see the target naturally and
instinctively build it into your play.

But an *internal* image of the target has a special function.
Rather than *think* about how hard to hit the ball, how far to
bring back the putter, or our follow through, just 'registering' the target seems to determine what we unconsciously
get on and do. It's the brain's instruction to go on to
automatic pilot. And you do it by *imagining* it - forming a
vivid mental picture whether it is within sight or not. Not
only does this allow you to keep your eye on the ball while
making a stroke, but it is also handy when the target you
want to hit is an imaginary one - say a few inches to the left
of the hole, or a particular place on the fairway that has no
obvious marker. Even in the short game, the flag can
become your dominant inner target by default when you
know you should actually be heading a couple of yards to
one side to compensate for the lie. Being able to construct your
own inner target overcomes this problem, but it needs to be
clear and strong - stronger than the image of what you want to
miss - in this case the flag, but perhaps the trees, lake or bunker.

Once you have clearly recorded the target in your mind,
you should be able to address the ball as normal and retain
the picture in your mind. You can take another look out
towards your target, but this is more to reinforce your inner
image than to check on the outer image - the landscape
tends not to change much and our sensory powers are
extraordinarily reliable if we can only learn to trust them.

Nick Price, once he has picked out a target, continues to
'see' it when he looks back to the ball. He dates his

consistency and success to the time he was able to commit himself to refusing to hit a shot unless his mind was locked on the target. Other players talk of having a sort of third eye which continues to see the target while they are addressing the ball. For other people the image of the target is not retained, but there is still the feeling of being locked into the target actually visualised prior to the shot.

## Muscle memory

You will have noticed how top golfers take one good look at their target and seem to make all the right decisions, then play a perfect shot based on that. This is partly because they have come to rely on muscle memory and can unconsciously draw on thousands of memories 'like' the shot in question, but also because they are able to visualise and hold their target while making the stroke. The very fact that they do this unconsciously underlines the extent to which they draw on these mental skills. You can lock any target into your mind, just as any successful shot you make can be recalled as a memory blueprint for future successes.

## Don't interfere

The way you picture your target will be personal and unique to you. Imagery can be in movies, as well as still pictures, of course. Many golfers see the ball starting on its trajectory, and others, like Ben Hogan, saw the whole shot, including the final rest of the ball in the visualised target position. This sort of dynamic visualisation (the journey of the ball as well as the destination) is especially helpful before or while addressing the ball rather than when making the swing. Often bizarre imagery is more effective than trying to be as authentic as possible. And you are not confined to visual imagery. The more senses you can use when setting internal targets - incorporating say sounds and feelings - the more realistic and vivid will be your representation. As with dreams, a vivid representation is more memorable - it has a bigger impact on the brain. Remember that *cybernetically*, that is, in terms of our natural, human goal-achieving system, only the target needs to be input. So you shouldn't try to interfere. All the rest - including the tiniest mid-swing adjustments - happens automatically. Making it dynamic rather than static just adds realism.

## Preparing for the big game

Mental rehearsal applies to any goal, such as reaching a single figure handicap, winning a tournament, or conquering a difficult hole. Or you can use it before an important game using 'armchair' visualisation the night before the game. It may be that you already have a system, both for preparing for important matches, and also for executing successful shots. In this case you may be able to use it better, develop it further, and in particular extend it to parts of your game with which you have not associated it. If not, start visualising and enter an exciting new subjective world that will pay big dividends in your game. This is the right brain side of goal achieving, and will harness all your subjective powers to improve your objective performance. Notice your new sense of purpose, and score improvement, as you apply the principles of well-formed outcomes, and the techniques of mental rehearsal. Once on the course, keep it simple: look at the target, look at the ball, and swing. Always have a purpose, an outcome, for every shot you make or round you play. Ask yourself where you are going in your golf, and in the other parts of your life as well.

# Masterstroke Question Clinic

**1. I don't seem to have any fun on the course any more. Why is this?**

If you really want fun, make sure it is clear on your hierarchy of goals. Then make sure that your other goals are compatible. For instance, does having fun come before or after (higher or lower on your outcome tree) other goals to do with your technical game? Would you be willing to give up the goal of having a perfect swing if that's what it means to keep the fun in the game? Perfectionism is a fun killer. And you are on a loser from the start as no two swings are identical. You can't reproduce a golf swing like a computer chip or a motorway bridge. Your beliefs, such as 'It's only a game' or 'I can enjoy myself whatever happens to the ball' or 'I'm not naturally competitive', may also affect your enjoyment of the game. You can change any unhelpful ones using the belief change exercise in Chapter 3.

**2. At the start of the season I made a commitment to get better, but nothing has happened. What has gone wrong? I did have a goal.**

Check back on your commitment and apply the tests of a well-formed outcome. Was your goal specific, measurable, realistic, etc.? Was it too big, or not sufficiently challenging? Then restate it in terms of your overall personal hierarchy of goals to be sure that it is congruent with the other things that are important to you. Get any 'ecology' right. Finally, start using your right brain to do some mental rehearsal to bring your commitment to life.

### 3. I want to play golf professionally but seem to be stuck at a handicap of 3. What do I do?

This is an important decision which is more than likely to have an effect on other parts of your life. Do the outcome tests carefully and pay attention to the ecology checks. What would I lose if I became a pro? What would change? How would other people in my life be affected? If there are unconscious but negative responses to these sorts of questions, you will have an inbuilt governor that stops you from reaching scratch, protecting you from negative consequences.

### 4. Why do I not look forward to playing any more?

Check back on the answer to the 'fun' question. It sounds like the same problem, and it can soon be put right once you sort out your personal priorities, and decide what you want to get out of the game.

### 5. My friend says I should do this, Nick Faldo says I should do that and Harvey Penick says something else. Whom do I believe?

First sort out what exactly you want to achieve and get out of the game as we have described. Decide on your own goals and keep your learning simple and enjoyable until you are ready for advice on specific matters. If you want to model a top player, fine, but don't blend your models; stick to one *for each learning objective*. And watch and copy rather than try to follow conflicting, unsolicited advice. Use the modelling techniques described in Chapter 5.

### 6. I've heard people talk about visualising the flight of the ball. I've never done this. Is it useful?

Seeing your target inside as we have described is important and people have all sorts of other imagery that helps to internalise their shots, including the trajectory, as did Ben

Hogan. Anyone can do this, and it then means you can practise effectively away from the course. These internal images - and sounds and feelings - can also be an important part of your pre-shot routine to help consistency.

### 7. *I am hitting the ball better but my scores and handicap have not yet come down. What can I do?*

Think targets and scores rather than swing mechanics. This might involve changes in how and what you practise, for instance. If your putting was as reliable as your drives, for example, more of your skill would convert into scores - that's just the way it works out. If, however, your technical skills are well balanced across the game, it is more likely that there are beliefs (Chapter 3) and goal priorities to sort out. Any such unconscious factors mysteriously affect final scores, however well you seem to be playing.

### 8. *When I hit a bad shot I seem to follow it with many others. Why?*

That's where we started the book - 'Don't let your last shot affect your present one.' Goal focus and a consistent set-up procedure to 'wipe the slate clean' is a good start, and you may have already thought about other things to try out from your goal-setting exercise. You will also learn how you can control the various kinds of mental baggage that can ruin your game. And you will learn how to practise what and how to *think* as well as what to do.

# 3 EMPOWERING BELIEFS

*N O W   T H A T* you have set clear goals, how do your beliefs affect your golf? If you believe 'I am weak on the greens' (or with sand shots, shots over water, teeing off, or whatever), will your negative belief affect your actual performance? Of course it will - it is likely to be a major factor. If you believe 'I don't have the right physical build to be a top golfer', or that you will never reach a certain handicap, will your belief limit your ultimate performance? It probably will, whatever the reality of your natural physique and the rationality of your conclusion. Self-beliefs act like governors on an engine that stop it going above a certain number of revolutions a minute. The power is there, but it is prevented from being used to the full.

Although you don't recite them like a personal creed each time you set foot on the golf course, or aren't even conscious of them, your beliefs play a vital part in all your performances. And the less aware of them you are, the more they are likely to play havoc with the goals you have set. You might say 'I really want to make a good shot, I really intend to get a better score, I will try my very hardest.' But a belief that says 'I'm going through a bad spell lately' or 'There's something not right about this new putter' will still do its job, acting just like a bunker in your mind, or any 'negative target' you really want to miss. In this chapter you will learn how to identify the beliefs that affect your game, and how to change them for more empowering ones, and better scores. First you need to understand something about how your beliefs operate and affect every shot you make and score you mark up.

## Your Personal Course Thermostat

Most of us are familiar with the way a shot we have just made influences how we perform on the next one. And from books and inspirational tapes we know the effect that self-belief can have on our performance, especially over the longer term. But the way we score a round, and especially the tendency for the last few holes to 'correct' any uncharacteristic scores in the early holes, starkly illustrates how beliefs can affect our game. Excellent front nine scores can be thrown away as our mind-body co-ordination, or lack of it, seems to prevent us from going on in the back nine - if our early score was extrapolated for the whole round - to what would be an *impossible* score. If your mind 'says' something is impossible, there is not much chance of achieving it. So we tend to gravitate to our personal score *comfort zone* (see Figure 3a on page 70), whatever we achieve on the early holes.

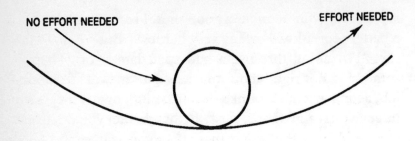

**Figure 3a** The Comfort Zone

For years Nick Price's game depended on how he played the first few holes. If they went well he went into a relaxed, confident frame of mind and proceeded to make a good score. And during those years he was certainly capable of good scores, with rounds in the mid sixties and lower. But inconsistency plagued him, and much of it was connected to his early holes performance. After a bad start, he might start trying to fix his swing as the round became increasingly erratic. Even worse for Price was to hit his approach shot close to the pin on the first hole, then miss the putt. This would set off a cycle of discouragement and negative belief that would account for his later poor scores. This is a common phenomenon with many club players. To some extent we might recover in the later holes, but by then it is too late. The mind has done its job.

Just as commonly, record scores on the way out are mysteriously eroded as we gravitate to what is a comfortable, 'believable' score. In this case, your self-belief acts as a sort of thermostat, and your final score has to comply with what is reasonable and believable, or, technically, as we saw in the previous chapter, what you can *imagine*. Once again, you only achieve what your mind can conceive, so clearly formed goals once again take on importance. As individual hole scores build up to a final round score, handicap and other higher level beliefs become more important as the mental thermostat clicks into operation. If this mental thermostat could be adjusted, just as the four-minute mile running barrier had to be lifted before physical records were broken, the same self-fulfilling system could work *for* you rather than against you. Logically, what you can do on the first nine you can do on the closing holes. What you can do on one weekend, you are physically capable of doing the next weekend. And, of far more dramatic significance to thousands of club players, what you can do physically in a friendly round you can do in an important tournament. What the body-mind partnership can do once, it can do again and again.

Golfers remain stuck for years in their 'comfort zone', subject to a mental thermostat as real as any physical swing defect. It's a mental game, and this involves taking control of your topsy-turvy world of ephemeral feelings or deep-rooted attitudes and beliefs, and starting to exercise your free will. When it comes to how you think, the choice really is yours. You can learn to believe what you want to believe, to program your thoughts for success rather than failure. You can adjust your personal score and handicap thermostat, and improve your performance in a quantum rather than marginal way.

## Getting Below The Surface

Beliefs are powerful. A single belief can affect several different goals or outcomes. 'I am not very co-ordinated,' for example, can play havoc with just about every part of your game. 'I'm a slicer,' or any other 'I'm . . .' category of belief is just as powerful. These beliefs are usually supported by a little army of lesser beliefs marching behind them, as well as actual 'failure' memories to back them up. But, however rational they seem, they are killers as far as your scores and handicap are concerned.

Beliefs, like goals, affect all our behaviour, and in a much bigger way than we are usually aware of. We naturally tend to concentrate on outside behaviour - because it is visible, and can be analysed. That is all that a playing partner or coach can see, and therefore make judgements and give 'advice' about. The whole of the mental side of golf, however, although we pay lip service to its importance, is harder to understand, and thus to do anything about. So it doesn't get anything like our time and attention. On top of this we assume we are stuck with our self-beliefs and unpredictable scores.

The underlying beliefs we have about ourselves and our abilities stay below the surface, doing their job very efficiently but out of sight and out of (conscious) mind. A useful metaphor is an iceberg, most of which is below the surface of the water. All we see is what is visible, but the Titanic danger to the unwary mariner is below the waterline, as in Figure 3b (see opposite).

This illustrates how performance, our scores and actual behaviour on the course are always affected by how we feel, our attitudes, values and beliefs. *Conscious* thoughts are just a tiny part of what goes on in the mind. We could never cope

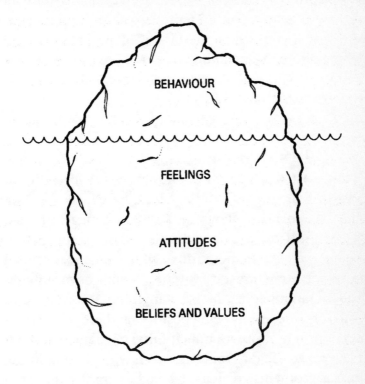

**Figure 3b** The Mental Iceberg

consciously, for example, with the hundreds of muscle movements and complex chemical happenings required in the simplest shot. These autopilot-type thoughts, as well as feelings and beliefs, go on below the surface. They all have a pecking order of importance, or impact on your goals.

## Feelings

Moment by moment *feelings* - just below the waterline - usually have an instant and quite direct effect. When you feel on top of the world it affects everything you do, and conversely when you are under the weather - for no apparent reason - your usual standards of performance can instantly fall. In this case you can sometimes psych yourself out of a mental trough. The next chapter deals specifically with controlling how you feel.

## Attitudes

Feelings, just like behaviour, however, can become habitual, so we can easily adopt *attitudes* which are more robust than volatile feelings, and thus are a bigger problem to deal with. If you get into the habit of seeing things from a gloomy, pessimistic point of view, for instance, you will soon adopt a pessimistic attitude. We all have different attitudes - about sport, life and anything else - hence we refer to some people as being positive, and others negative, some helpful and others unhelpful. The right attitude in golf can make the difference between winning and losing. At critical moments - which is when the winning and losing happens - it is worth a dozen lessons analysing your swing.

## Beliefs

Attitudes in turn can become beliefs - about people, yourself, the game of golf or the world. If you are a pessimist you are more likely to believe you will lose in an important match, or will not make it as a professional, or never make anything of your life, than an optimist - however your actual experience and abilities compare to those of your optimistic colleague. These beliefs are powerful long-term drivers that affect your motivation and performance.

It's one iceberg - the behaviour you can see and analyse, and everything below the surface you are not even aware of. That's the mind-body system. But it is what goes on below the surface that holds the key to big improvements in your game.

## Hierarchy Of Beliefs And Values

The whole system forms a sort of hierarchy, just like your personal goals, with beliefs and values at many levels supporting your actual behaviour. Little beliefs (like 'I'm slicing today') support bigger ones (like 'I'm a slicer'), which in turn might be underpinned by 'I have poor co-ordination', then, in turn, perhaps, 'I don't have the right build for golf.' Before you realise it, maybe, way down towards the bottom of the submerged iceberg, beliefs like 'I'm generally a loser in life' or 'I've never had much luck on my side' take over. As surely as icebergs float, your belief will turn into reality.

Up nearer the surface your feelings one weekend might be that you are pretty sick about having sliced the ball a couple of times. And, sure enough, your next shot confirms you are right to feel that way, and to believe all the things you believe about yourself . The problem is no longer just in the mind. Your over-trying and tense muscles make sure you are *really* uncoordinated. The plain fact is that actual behaviour is *inextricably linked* to all the thought processes that go on in the submerged iceberg of your mind. Your mind-body is one system, just as an iceberg is a single block of ice.

## *Self-fulfilling downward spiral*

Common, apparently harmless self-beliefs can form a vicious downward spiral of poor performance. And it can start from a couple of random slices, or any other rogue behaviour.

I'm slicing today
    I feel sick about that shot
        I'm a slicer
            I lack co-ordination
                It's just like me
                    I'm no good at golf
                        I'm a loser

**Figure 3c** The Stairway to Failure

A self-fulfilling downward spiral is at work. So a random lousy stroke, or the thoughtless comment of a relative or teacher can grow into a deeply held, disempowering self-belief. A fact becomes an opinion. A feeling is supported by attitudes and beliefs ('Trust me to do that again!'), which affect future behaviour, which in turn reinforces the belief. Hence the ever-comforting thought 'I told you so.' A harmless shot above the surface is *interpreted* below. If things are in order below the surface you have got everything going for you when it comes to actual performance. In particular, you become more consistent.

# The Case For Empowering Beliefs

There are good reasons why we need to give a lot more attention to what happens in the mind, and especially at the level of self-beliefs.

1. There is more *leverage* at this level. This means that a relatively small change - say to a single belief or attitude - can have a very big effect. A positive, confident attitude, for instance, can improve your performance a lot more than concentrating on the mechanics of your swing. Several above-the-surface behaviours can be influenced by that one attitude. Deeper down, beliefs such as 'I have a natural instinct for the game', 'I can make sound judgements when in difficulty', or 'I respond well to pressure' can have a fundamental effect on every kind of shot, and your whole game. There is even more leverage.

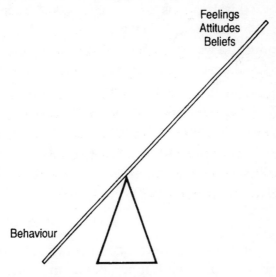

**Figure 3d** Mental Leverage

All sorts of technical weaknesses can be offset by strengths in this area of controlling beliefs, so it's a wise investment of your attention. This is where you need to concentrate if you want to seriously reduce your handicap.

2. Leverage saves effort. Although this might be hard to accept if you are new to the way beliefs and thought processes work, it is actually a lot *easier* to make changes when you start with the mental side. This is not because mental habits are any easier to change *per se* than physical ones - they operate under the same system, and you cannot separate mind and body - but because so little has usually been done in the mental dimension that the potential winnings are far greater. Just like when a person who is very unfit starts to do proper exercises and follows a correct diet, the improvement can be quite dramatic. The belief change process you will learn is also enjoyable.

3. Much of this happens *unconsciously*, so much of our performance happens by default - we don't know what is happening and we certainly don't have control. External behaviour, because it is so visible, and amenable to analysis - like the swing - gets all our attention, whether or not it is the real problem. Conversely, the mental side is ignored. Out of sight may be out of *conscious* mind, but very much part of our *unconscious* mind. The outcome tests in the previous chapter help to bring both intentions and beliefs *to the surface*, so that you can do something about them.

These are good reasons to start concentrating more on the beliefs and attitudes that happen below the surface. First you need to identify them, then, if necessary, change them.

# Getting To Know Your Inner Interpreter

The relationship between what goes on in your mind and your actual performance is so strong and self-fulfilling that you have to deal with your beliefs radically. Rather than tweaking them here and there as you might your swing, some negative beliefs have to be booted out of your life without mercy. Having no rational basis (as is likely to be the case), and having short-changed you for so long, you will in any case be well rid of them. In this way, rather than just tackling physical behaviour, which usually recurs, you can completely reverse a negative, downward spiral of performance, make big inroads into your handicap, and get more pleasure out of your golf into the bargain. But behaviour and beliefs are like two sides of the same coin: what you do and what you think about what you've done. It's all to do with how you *interpret* your behaviour.

## *Making excuses*

How you interpret your present behaviour will influence your future behaviour. For instance, let's say you make a shot way off to your left, into the rough, overcompensating for a hazard on the right. You can say, 'That's not like me, I'll not do that again in a hurry,' or words to that effect. Alternatively, you might say to yourself, 'Trust me to do that. I always overdo things.' The chances are that with the first interpretation you are more likely to make a better shot next time, having put the 'fluke' right out of your mind. With the second interpretation, however, the tendency is for the interpretation to be *acted upon* - you fulfil your belief.

Your next shot, or one a few strokes ahead, will then confirm and further strengthen your interpretation.

This interpreting of behaviour happens automatically as part of the feedback in the four-part masterstroke cycle we met in the first chapter. NLP refers to our interpretations as *excuses*. As well as using sensory acuity to know whether to adjust to the right or left, or softer or harder, we *filter* the feedback according to our feelings, attitudes, and beliefs - and all this happens below the surface of outward behaviour. Nevertheless this *filtered representation* is what determines how we learn and what we will tend to do next. So in golf as in anything else you are no better than your excuses. You have to live with your own interpretations.

## Turning excuses into facts

These interpretations, or excuses, may have little bearing on the facts. Any statistical analysis around the time that these positive or negative interpretations were established, for example, might show that neither golfer displayed any significant difference either way. Only their *interpretation* differed - perhaps one person is more optimistic than the other in everyday life, or maybe they had very different upbringings, or one was just having a bad day. Their differing perceptions and feelings, however, inevitably affected their subsequent performance. In due course, *actual* performance will substantiate even the most irrational interpretation.

In other words, *excuses turn into facts* - real behaviour. So we can always say 'I told you so,' 'I was right all along.' That is the strange logic of self-fulfilling beliefs and interpretations, and another example of the close, two-way, mind-body relationship. The good news is that you can interpret whatever you do *in any way you like*.

Although we don't usually express them, we have an interpretation for each behaviour - an excuse, if you like, for every shot we play, in the game of life as well as in golf. And those interpretations - basically what goes on in our minds - become the self-fulfilling basis for further behaviour.

Excuses can be empowering as well as disempowering. A duff shot can just as easily be labelled a 'fluke' as 'typical'. The really damaging kind are the permanent or all-pervasive excuses such as 'I *always* do that' or 'I *never* do so-and-so' - factually nonsense, but accepted slavishly by the brain. The trick is to make your positive excuses just as all-pervasive. Start to interpret all your behaviour in a way that supports rather than wrecks your actual performance, and that will tend to make you feel better rather than worse about your next shot or round. Like goals and beliefs, these excuses operate at every level. If you want to lower your golf handicap, keep fit, or have more fun in life you can interpret your behaviour in a way that is helpful rather than a hindrance to each specific goal. You can think what you like, but it will affect whatever you do and achieve.

# The NLP Model

The basic NLP model (shown in Figure 3e on page 82) explains how these beliefs, values and attitudes have such an effect on all our behaviour. Each of our five senses are *filtered* before they are recorded on the brain to become meaning, or understanding. And these filters are the feelings, values and beliefs we have already discussed.

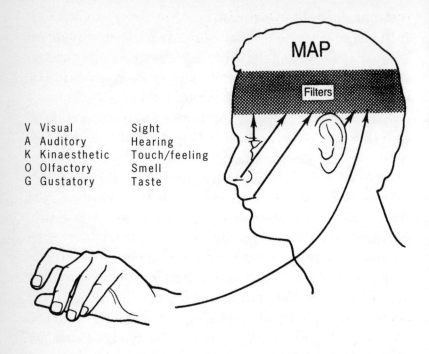

V  Visual          Sight
A  Auditory        Hearing
K  Kinaesthetic    Touch/feeling
O  Olfactory       Smell
G  Gustatory       Taste

**Figure 3e** The NLP Model

This explains why different people can place very different meanings on the same outside events or circumstances. One person, for example, is happy about what makes another person sad. Our unique background, education and upbringing explain the great differences in the way we perceive things, and the values and beliefs we hold. 'Reality' is therefore different for every person - we each have our own version. And, humbling though it is, none of us knows true reality, in that everything that enters our brain through the five sensual receptors goes through these perceptual filters. This results in our different interpretations, or representations - as we have seen, the excuses we make - and thus our different, usually highly individual, behaviour.

In one sense we are stuck with this. You can't undo all your personal history, and wipe out the billions of electro-chemical brain recordings that make you think and act the way you do. They are what make you uniquely you. But you *can* change how you think *now*, including what you think about the past and the future. You are in control. If you want to look on something optimistically, rather than expecting the worst, you are free to do that - whatever your upbringing, education, IQ or DNA. The chances are you could make an argument either way if it really was a matter of argument. If you are looking for excuses for failure, you will soon find them - there are plenty around. But if you want to believe that you can do better in some area of your life - and there are countless volumes of biographies to support such a self-belief - you are free to believe it. Over a period we do indeed change our values and beliefs as we acquire knowledge, watch and meet other people, and have more experience of life. But there are ways to quickly change thought processes - including beliefs - so that they fit better with your present purposes. Get your unique mental filter working for you rather than against you, and see your scores come down.

## Golf Self-Belief

As far as your golf is concerned, the criterion for a belief should be: On balance, is this helping me to achieve my objectives in the game, or hindering me? Your objectives, as you saw in the previous chapter, might include a straight-forward drop in your handicap, or they might be more specific, such as mastering a particular stroke or getting over a hang-up about a troublesome course or hole. Or you might want to get more enjoyment out of the game, or get and stay fit, or your goal might be to do with relationships or your career. You decide what you want. It is in the context of *what you want* that beliefs become important. If you believe you can never break 80 and are happy with your lot, your belief is congruent with what you want. If, on the other hand, you want to play off scratch, such a belief will almost certainly be a psychological barrier to everything you attempt. Self-beliefs are either friends or foes, empowering or disempowering, helping or hindering you in achieving what you want. But they are *your* beliefs - nobody else's - so you can form them, change them, and use them as you like. The following exercises show you exactly how.

# Exercise: Identifying Negative Beliefs

To play better golf you need to identify and change any beliefs that are hindering you from fulfilling your true potential. This is the process you will follow. First identify the beliefs that hinder you from achieving your golfing objectives. Next choose the top three offenders. Then apply the specific belief change program that is described in detail below.

As far as identifying negative beliefs or hang-ups is concerned, we have already used some as examples, but here are some more:

○ My putter's not right.

○ I naturally hook the ball.

○ I can't rise to the big occasion.

○ I can't play out of sand.

○ My basic swing's no good.

○ I always play the last three holes badly.

○ I am terrified on the first tee if anybody is watching.

○ I am hopeless at chipping.

○ I can't slow my swing down.

○ I can't control my temper.

○ I feel inadequate when I play with better players.

○ I dread playing out of a bunker.

○ I'm no good on fast greens.

○ I'm no good on slow greens.

○ I can't play well when it's wet or windy.

○ I never play well when I really want to.

○ I was never good at sports.

○ My new grip feels terrible.

○ Water hazards terrify me.

Make your own list. Be honest with yourself, and be prepared to dig deep, because, as we have seen, some of these operate below the surface of consciousness. Note also that self-beliefs are not events or behaviour, but what we *think* about the behaviour or event. They are not usually the reality of what we are or can do, but what we *think* we can do, or think we are. They can be about things (such as a club, or the local greens), people (such as the partner who makes you nervous), the world in general, or yourself.

As it happens, self-beliefs are the best place to start, not least because you can always do something about them if you really want to. We are often the last to identify our own negative beliefs, so you might have to give this exercise a little thought. A friend might quickly remind you of what you have said from time to time and ways you have acted that indicate your beliefs. Of course you will probably have positive as well as negative beliefs, and the rule with positive beliefs is simple - leave well alone. They will carry on serving you well.

## *Exercise:*
## *Changing a Belief*

Here is one technique to change a disempowering belief. It is based on the fact that there is a two-way relationship between our beliefs and our behaviour. Beliefs affect our behaviour, but our behaviour in turn affects our beliefs. This technique uses behaviour, but rather than tackling external behaviour - the visible part of the iceberg, if you like - it *creates* behaviour internally to support your belief.

### 1. Identify the disempowering belief
First identify the self-belief you would like to change. Go for one that is not too general (like 'I am a loser' or 'I am usually unlucky') or not too specific (like 'I always go to pieces at the twelfth hole on so-and-so course on Saturdays'). But a belief about a particular kind of shot, a nuisance habit you have developed, how you react to competition, or your handicap level ('I can't see myself breaking into single figures,' for instance) is fine for this

purpose. Write your belief down so that it is quite clear to you.

## 2. Decide on an empowering replacement belief

You then need a replacement belief. All your beliefs have served you well in their own way, as sort of survival rules. Your mind does not like a vacuum, so state the belief you would like to replace the disempowering one, and again write it down. This might be a straight reversal, such as 'I am naturally co-ordinated,' rather than 'I lack co-ordination,' or 'I am well capable of single figures' in the handicap example. Or you might go for something a bit more than just reversing what you are losing, such as 'I am naturally co-ordinated, and can focus my whole mind and body on the immediate shot' or 'I am well capable of single figures, and have the mental control to go a lot further in golf.' Choose carefully, as a fundamental belief change has more potential power than a new set of clubs or many hours of technical tuition.

## 3. Choose three supporting behaviours

Then think of three behaviours that illustrate your positive belief - that is, things you would actually do if you really believed what you want to believe. These might be specific shots, on a familiar course, say, that confirm your belief - a perfect recovery shot, a masterly bunker shot, an eagle on the disastrous seventeenth, or whatever. Or they might be experiences such as receiving a trophy or other accolade of success, such as the hearty congratulations of friends at the end of a successful round or match. They may either be based on memories - suitably adjusted as you wish - or just imagined as future happenings. Choose behaviours that can be realistically *imagined* using all your inner senses - sights, sounds and feelings - which act as *evidence* of the truth of your belief.

## 4. Mentally rehearse your new behaviours

Using your three examples, *mentally rehearse* each one in vivid detail; see yourself in your mental picture excelling in whatever way you want to. Initially stay outside the action, so that you see yourself as if watching from outside (this is termed 'dissociated'). If you are not completely happy with your new performance, run through it again and fine-tune it wherever you wish, until it perfectly confirms your positive belief. Then put yourself right inside, and experience everything, including the reactions of other people, this time seeing things through your own eyes (termed 'associated'). Enjoy all the surrounding feelings and emotions, including the reactions of friends or playing partners, that accompany your success. By repeating the visualisation as a form of mental practice, you will *create* the necessary internal behaviour that will support your new belief.

Applying this technique to your top three offending negative beliefs, you will remove long-standing barriers that will free you mentally to make better scores. Do this in conjunction with the goal-setting exercise in the previous chapter - everything you have learnt so far remains valid as you learn something new.

The above is just one example of a belief change technique. A longer technique, described in Harry Alder's book *NLP for Managers* (Piatkus), makes the change through several stages, and may be more effective in the case of particularly long-standing, major beliefs.

# *A word about mental rehearsal*

You used mental rehearsal as a way to internalise your goals and register them in your success 'system'. It also has an important neurological effect which brings about the belief change. At one level, the brain does not know the difference between a vividly imagined event and the real thing, so the mental imagery acts like real experience - as if you had actually experienced the behaviour. It's much like daydreaming, or true dreaming, which can be just as real as so-called reality, with similar effects on both your emotions and physiology, such as blood pressure and breathing. The internally 'represented' behaviour supports your new belief, and there is now *congruence* between how you see yourself and how you behave.

This is a technique for mental practice which is very different to physical practice, both of which you will meet in Chapter 6. With physical practice, the chances are that you will miss more than you ever hit. That is just a fact of life, and is not confined to golf, but the result is that you might further compound your negative self-belief. This explains why people do not get the improvement they expect out of long practice sessions, and sometimes even go backwards. Mental practice, on the other hand, need not involve failures, or misses. So the experience of success is just the sort you need, both to verify your new belief, and also to give you the confidence that *may* eventually come from a succession of successful golf experiences, but often eludes us even after many years in the game.

For these mental techniques to work, you need to *trust* your mind, and in particular accept its tendency to treat inner experience in a similar way to external experience. This need not be a problem once you understand that sights and sounds are eventually converted into electro-chemical 'firings', in the brain, of the same sort as when you recall any experience (remember) or create sensory experiences internally (imagine). Using computer analogy, different input devices may be used, but once inside, the data are processed and reprocessed in the same way. But you cannot erase 'failure' memories in the way that you can wipe a computer hard disk clean. So you need to counterbalance negative 'recordings' with positive, success mind-recordings. The more you mentally practise the behaviours that reinforce your desired belief, and the more realistic the imagery, the more effective the belief change will be.

## Feeling better

Just as with physical skills, mental skills involve learning and practice. But mental rehearsal can be very enjoyable, as success of any kind usually is. So, as well as changing beliefs, which now have to fit your new 'experience', you will find that you also *feel* better. This is a bonus from each belief change, and your times of mental rehearsal. Not least, you feel good about operating at a level you should have been capable of all along. And the *actual* improvement that inevitably follows a belief change of this sort brings its own good feelings, as well as further confirming your new belief, and establishing the upward spiral of performance. All you have done is throw off the irrational, historical beliefs that were established by random negative interpretations some time in the past, and started to do, consistently, what you are well capable of doing. It's just a matter of mental reprogramming. Or, using an earlier analogy, you have simply turned off the engine governor, so you can now reach the performance you were designed to reach.

For this exercise you can start with three disempowering

beliefs, but you can later apply the technique to as many as you like as you become more skilled. Any one of them might bring about a surprising hike in your performance. Similarly, the more supporting behaviours you can use in your mental rehearsal for each new belief, provided they can be vividly imagined, the stronger will be your new belief. Then success will breed success. Your sights will be raised, and a positive motivating handicap target will have to be replaced with one that is even more challenging, but with beliefs to support it.

You can add non-golf beliefs to your list, as these are likely to play a part somewhere in your personal hierarchy of beliefs. The process is the same. This will provide a further 'ecology' check to your outcomes, so that you establish congruence between your golf activities and other important parts of your life.

# Masterstroke Question Clinic

### 1. *I play better for a while when I get a new set of clubs, then go back to normal. Why is this?*

This just reinforces how a simple belief, in this case in your new clubs, can change your whole performance. Now that you know how to set new beliefs you may want to fix some that are not so dependent on tools, or any external factors. A simple replacement belief that attitude is more important than equipment, or that clubs become *more* effective over time (like a Stradivarius violin) will probably do the trick. One of your supporting behaviours might be visualising a round with a couple of ancient irons and making a record score - exercise your imagination!

Alternatively it is possible to *imagine* you are playing with a new club, even after its newness wears off, thus recreating the positive association that helped your game for a while. The only rule is what works for you.

### 2. *I sometimes play a great front nine, then lose it on the back nine.*

This is the comfort zone or thermostat problem I described at the beginning of the chapter. You are settling into a final score your personal belief system can live with. A new belief, set at a lower handicap, backed by realistic supporting behaviour visualisation, will change your personal thermostat. In effect you will *act as if* you were playing off a lower handicap. So your unconscious goal-belief will always be ahead of your present performance level, which is vital if you are continuously to improve. Also, check back on the goal-setting size criterion in Chapter 2. Make sure your score objectives stretch you, and that your self-beliefs - which you can now change as you wish - are congruent with them.

### 3. *I always play my favourite course well. Why is this?*

This is a bit like the new club effect. It's what you believe and feel about it. Again, fix your beliefs so they are not dependent on outside circumstances or conditions. Have a look at Chapter 6 on practice, for tips about preparing for non-familiar situations. But ideally your mental control applies shot by shot, and in the next chapter you will learn a bit more about how to control your attitude and feelings in any circumstances.

**4. I was never any good at sports at school. Can I be good at golf?**

Yes, you can be. And a belief change about your general sports capability would be a great start. Use the belief change exercise. You might also like to look out for biographies of late starters. Everybody is good at something, and aspects of these personal 'success strategies' (what is happening in your mind, for instance, when you do well in a non-sport activity) are transferable to your golf.

**5. After the first round of a two-day tournament I was leading, then had a terrible second round. Why?**

This is another form of the 'back nine' problem we described. Such inconsistency is inevitable without a solid mental game, which means your goals, beliefs and state of mind are congruent. Use the technique above to up your personal tournament thermostat.

**6. Why do I feel so uncomfortable playing with low handicap golfers?**

Players far worse than you feel the very opposite, so this is just a matter of self-belief, which you can change if you want to. Think about all the things you can do better than them. And take advantage of all the learning opportunities. With the right mental approach you can soon overtake them in any case.

**7. Since I turned professional and I have unlimited time to practise, my game has got worse. Why?**

Forgetting the time you now have, it is common to face self-belief problems on the important transition to professional status, in which the pressures are different. So check out everything above on beliefs, as well as making out a full hierarchy of goals as described in the previous chapter. On going professional many people start doing things differently, such as changing their swing, almost for the sake of it, and thus go backward. There are enough changes to cope with without creating them. Time management is important, and quality rather than quantity in practice is what matters. The chances are you are not practising *mentally* much, or that the *weighting* of your practice is not geared to scores - see Chapter 6 on practice.

### 8. I feel I have to win at golf to enjoy it. Why?

This might be competitiveness or perfectionism, but it is all too common. Sooner or later you will have to accept that there will always be somebody out there who can beat you, but that doesn't mean you can't enjoy the game or that your self-esteem need be affected. You may sort it out personally by going through the outcome tests in Chapter 2. A *dynamic* goal - like getting better, against your own standards, over a period - rather than a static, absolute goal - allows you to win every time, whatever the competition. Paradoxically, the more you focus on your goals (destination), the process (journey) - which is playing the game - becomes more important and enjoyable.

### 9. How can I tell whether an error is psychological or physical?

There may not be an either/or answer, as we are one 'system'. However, a fault that increases with pressure is likely to be psychological. Similarly, if the errors are worse on the course than in practice conditions, you can be sure the mind is up to something. Clearly, if you get mad after three putting and sky your next shot, it is psychological. Often after a duff shot you will recall coming to it with negative thoughts, and such thoughts invariably account for the shot.

# 4 GETTING INTO THE PLAYING STATE OF MIND

$YOU\ SHOULD$ now have clear, positive goals, and beliefs that support them. But perhaps you are still affected by whom you are playing with, the state of the course, or whatever, or maybe you have difficulty maintaining your focus, staying calm, or controlling your nerves. Sometimes you simply don't *feel* right, for no apparent reason, and your performance drops - it's just one of those days.

Bobby Jones was renowned for his reliable, repetitive technique which secured many major titles but he admitted that, although his skill constantly got him into a commanding position, it seemed that on many occasions his temperament took over and he squandered opportunities to win more titles. Henry Cotton, another all-time great, also confesses that for years his efforts to win the British Open were undermined by his fickle temperament. In his case the Open proved to be a particular mental hurdle. For you it may be a club tournament or some other competitive event, the condition of the greens, a competitor who gets under your skin, or whatever. For Harry Vardon, temperament was an asset. He was a quiet, placid man and proved to be a dangerous, patient rival who could never be counted out. This chapter covers the crucial golfing problem of being in the right state of mind.

## Creating Feelings That Empower

Let's start by linking how we feel with the goals we set.

### *Exercise:*
### *Focus on What You Want*

Focusing on what you want rather than what you don't want actually affects how you feel, so you can easily do something about it. Here's a simple exercise. First, think about something you *don't* want - maybe to do with your golf, but for this exercise it could be to do with any aspect of your life. Imagine it actually happening - what you would see, hear and especially how you would feel. Draw on memories where possible to make it more realistic. Write down some words that describe how you feel about what you have imagined - the thing going wrong, the embarrassment maybe, or the disappointment. Words like pain, frustration, fear, nervousness, anger are the sort that will probably describe how you feel about something happening that you did not want. Notice particularly how your feelings change when you imagine this happening - and how quickly the change happened.

Now think about something you *do* want, and again experience vividly the sights, sounds and feelings associated with it. 'Pre-live' the experience, and note again how you feel. This time the words that come to mind might be pleasure, fulfilment, relief, pride, contentment, and so on - scribble them down as they occur to you. Notice how good you now feel, and how easily the change occurred when you visualised the positive outcomes. You can check this further by using more examples. With practice, and careful choice of memories and motivating desires, you will be able to change how you feel instantly.

Now ask yourself the common-sense question: Which state of mind is more likely to help actually bring about my goal? Obviously the positive feelings are the most useful, and motivating. We achieve more, learn better, and have more pleasure when we are pursuing a worthwhile, positive outcome. By visualising your outcomes in a positive rather than a negative way - what you want rather than what you don't want - you can change how you feel and increase your chances of success.

## Bunkers in the mind

Now apply this to any aspect of your golf. Does the image of the ball landing exactly where you want it to give a *better feeling* than the images of the obstacles you want to avoid, with all their past memories and negative associations? And which sort of feeling is the most empowering - is most likely to help you reach your target? A young 4-handicap friend described what he thinks about when he prepares for a shot. He explained that if he has not done well on the last shot, he tends to think about what went wrong and what to avoid, perhaps also remembering other similar occasions when that situation or shot got him into trouble. But if he has done well on the previous shot, and perhaps the last few, he does not worry about the obstacles, but just makes his shot, seeing the desired trajectory of the ball before he hits it. I then asked him to think back about how his success rate compared as between shots for which he thought about what to miss, and those he thought about positively. His answer was that far more of the shots he thought about positively actually came off - and his reply is typical. In other words, it made an *actual difference* whether he thought about his target or goal in positive or negative imagery. Given any thought at all, this of course is obvious, yet it remains one of the main cases of inconsistency. Common sense is not too common. This underlines the importance of  the 'positive' test you applied to your outcomes.

However natural it seems to be affected by your immediately preceding performance, the fact is that you can change how you feel if you want to - as the last simple exercise proved. You are free to think whatever you want to think, so it makes sense to think positive, empowering thoughts. All my young, talented golfer friend changed was his thinking, but he got better results than untold hours of practice at the many 'offending' shots.

The same mental strategy can be used, not just to counteract a shot you want to forget, but to neutralise any negative feeling - perhaps concerning your partner, equipment, the weather, or something happening at work - that might rob you of the results you are capable of. By mentally rehearsing a positive outcome, you will feel the way you would if it actually happened. This is the very state of mind you need, of course, for the actual shot. And you can create such a state of mind *just by thinking* - as you did earlier when thinking about positive and negative goals.

## Aligning how you feel with what you want

Good golf is all about being in the right state of mind. You may need confidence, or a feeling of calmness, or maybe a 'couldn't care less' attitude. This is a big part of the mental game, and it is where you will get the edge, and where the big improvements are likely to come. You have just made a start by noticing the difference between fixing an outcome positively or negatively.

The size of your goal, which is one of the outcome tests we met in Chapter 2, might also affect the way you feel. For instance, a goal that is set too high can create panic or a mental blanking off, while one that is too low might create boredom and lack of concentration. In either case you don't feel right, so your muscles are likely to be tense and you won't perform as you are able. The experience of 'flow', or mastery, however, associated with the right size of goal that is challenging and highly motivating, is the mental state that consistently produces the best results. The sensory evidence you gave your goals also enables right brain imagery which affects how you feel. Positive, motivating, sensory-based goals are an essential part of your automatic success system, and thus a vital ingredient in any 'flow' type behaviour. So you can influence how you feel, and thus how you perform, by the way you go about setting and internalising your goals. Each of the tests we described, besides reinforcing your inner target, helps you to feel confident and positive - the state you need to consistently score well.

## Winning strategies

Visualising your shot outcome is just one example of a *strategy* - a series of sensory representations that bring about your desired outcome. It might well have involved some inner dialogue, unique imagery, music, or a physical feeling. The golfer we referred to earlier visualised the initial trajectory of the ball as his positive pre-shot imagery. Others see the ball landing and coming to rest. These are just mental programs, and you are free to use any mental 'software' you like, to see if it helps. What works for you may not work as well for the next person.

The point is that a winning strategy can produce winning results. It is your mental blueprint for success and, as we have seen, is the secret of unconscious, or natural competence. If you are willing to trust the 'system', every shot will get the best your mind-body partnership is able to give -

whatever has gone before, or whatever may follow.

Remember that if you have done something once, you can do it again and again. Trusting your inbuilt system makes no less sense than sticking to your special recipe for a soufflé or getting a shave and shower in four minutes. You don't for a moment doubt your ability to carry out these habitual tasks. The key to unlock this consistency in golf is not your physical condition or technical knowledge, but a trusting, confident state of mind - a mental strategy for success.

## Pre-shot routine

A consistent pre-shot routine is an invaluable success strategy for a golfer. The moments before each shot are when you are getting into the right state of mind. This is when you will relax, get focused and empty your mind of negative thoughts, internalise your target, and apply successful 'anchors' that recall winning shots or an empowering state of mind. In fact the outcome of your shot is largely determined before you hit the ball.

The content of your routine is not nearly as important as the fact that you have one, and that it is repetitive, consistent, and instinctive - you do it without thinking. Unlike the fundamental skills we shall look at in the next chapter, there is no standard pre-shot routine, with its physical and mental idiosyncrasies. Wiggles, waggles, shakes and shuffles - if they help to get you relaxed and focused, even in pressure situations, they are doing their job. But routine is the name of this particular game. Seve Ballesteros says that the more we ingrain a routine of setting up by repeatedly rehearsing our procedures on the driving range and in casual play, the less we'll be likely to step out of line when it really matters. Greg Norman prefers a brisk pace, and argues that a lot of fiddling and fidgeting during the address can mean you are second-guessing at a time when you should be absolutely confident and ready to swing. Some argue differently, which illustrates that the pre-shot routine, although functional and indispensable, tends to reflect different personality traits. But it can certainly be the key to superlative play. Bob Tway comments that if you watch someone playing 'in the zone', he or she is doing everything the same - address, tempo, mannerisms. There is a sort of comfort in routine that takes the pressure out of any situation.

Although many mental rehearsal techniques can be applied, say, the day before an important match, many of the principles and techniques you will learn happen in these important moments before each shot. There is certainly plenty to achieve, and you may have to block from your mind the horror shot you have just played, bad memories of the particular hole you are facing, or the thought of winning - or losing - the round, as well as setting your clear target and getting mentally and physically composed. Fortunately all this is easy once it becomes routine. And the secret of routine is repetition - practice. It follows that your practice sessions should incorporate your pre-shot routine, or, as you will see in Chapter 6 on practice, you will learn to be good at practice but unable to transfer your skills to the game.

A sound pre-shot routine helps in a multitude of ways, and you will not advance far in the game without developing your own, unique strategy. Some of the benefits are:

○ you will be more relaxed and deflect anxiety;

○ you will be more decisive;

○ you will shut out past, future, and any negative thoughts;

○ you will have familiar activities to resort to under pressure;

○ you can make all your mental and physical preparation instinctive;

○ it prevents you from rushing a shot;

○ it engages your muscle memories on which unconscious actions are based;

○ it acts as a check list for total shot preparation;

○ it helps develop a sound tempo;

○ it helps you to anchor confidence and trust in your strokes;

○ it is your opportunity to physically and mentally rehearse every stroke;

○ it allows you to express your personality and strengthen your self-belief;

○ it produces consistency in your shot-making; and

○ it allows you take and maintain full control.

You can, of course, have different routines for full shots, short shots, and putting, although some of the content may be common to every situation. And you need not become so dependent on your pre-shot routine that if for any reason you are unable to use it, or don't follow it perfectly, you will hit a bad shot. The secret is to be consistent rather than compulsive, instinctive rather than robotic. It is just a helpful device, but a very important one.

# Calling Up Confidence

The way you think about your shot, hole, or game - the imagery, feelings, and any structure in your mind - affects the actual outcome.  This is not mind over matter. It is much simpler. The mind is connected to the body and what your body does determines what happens to the ball. By understanding, then taking control of this intricate mind-body partnership - you are the boss - you can begin to do consistently what you need to do. Decide what state of mind will empower you to achieve your specific outcomes, and use NLP technology to make the changes. Here is a simple trial technique to call up confidence, or any other state you need, as you approach a shot.

1. Remember a specific time and place when you had the state you now want.

2. Relive that experience, enjoying recreating the sights, sounds and feelings as vividly as you can.

3. Concentrate on what was going through your mind both as you were approaching the shot and also as you were carrying it out.

4. As the feeling intensifies proceed to make your shot.

Later you will learn how to anchor these states, and be able to get into them instantly, and also how to develop your visualising skill to use in other ways. If you are new to golf and cannot recollect positive memories to draw on, you can recall other activities in which you had the right state of mind. Confidence, calmness, etc. are common to all sorts of sports and activities. Otherwise you can choose a favourite golfer and imagine you are them playing the shot.

## Creating a blueprint for success

Your mental 'representation' of the successful outcome or goal acts as a blueprint for what becomes reality. The blueprint includes what you do (the 'automatic' skill) and the state you are in. In terms of the four-part masterstroke model, the way you *think* about your goal determines the system's target, without which - whatever your technical skills, or however hard you try - the inbuilt system will flounder. By changing your thinking, first consciously, and then by allowing mental habits to develop - just as with tying your shoelaces or driving a car - you can instruct the system to do what it is designed to do. Top golfers have identified indecision as one of the biggest problems in the game. Indecision is a neurological state in which your representation of what you want to achieve - the sights, sounds and feelings in your mind - is not clear. Fuzzy thinking means indecision and erratic shot-making. A clear instruction, in the form of vivid imagery, is your blueprint for success.

# Mental Rehearsal For Controlling How You Feel

You have already met mental rehearsal, both for visualising outcomes and changing beliefs. It is also the basic technique for controlling how you feel. One of the principles we met earlier was that at one level the mind does not seem to know the difference between clearly imagined images, and the real thing. This means, for example, that by clearly imagining something you can *feel* the way you would if it actually happened. We all experience this when dreaming about a future holiday, imagining what it will be like to drive our new car, or anticipating some future pleasure. In terms of golf, it means that you can create mentally a few super shots, or rounds, or win the odd tournament, and feel great. And these feelings can be used to influence future behaviour - they are self-fulfilling. Real or imagined success makes us feel better, and the better feeling translates into yet more success. Worry is just a negative form of mental rehearsal. So we are all familiar with the process, although it usually happens by default, rather than under our control. Mental rehearsal can help you in several ways to get into the right state of mind.

○ It helps to ***internalise a goal*** - to make it real as far as the brain is concerned. You see, hear and feel the outcome you want, so that it becomes *experience*. You then *expect* it to happen.

○ You are ***motivated*** towards a mental image just as you are towards a real, attractive image. Hence the extraordinary power of what we refer to as a dream or burning ambition. Daydreaming, provided it is directed towards well-formed outcomes, as we discussed in Chapter 2, is thus a very productive pastime.

○ It acts as the ***target instruction*** for your unconscious goal achieving system. It becomes the blueprint of success, if you like, or a programmed instruction as applied to a computer. It can be the basis of 'flow', or unconscious competence.

○ It helps you to ***control how you feel,*** by changing how you represent things. You can *create* feelings by conscious visualisation.

○ It is a form of ***mental practice***, increasing your mental acuity and control over how you feel, and giving you the confidence that comes from repeated success. It supplements physical practice, and has its own special characteristics, as you will learn in Chapter 6.

○ As you saw in the simple exercise earlier, it can help to induce ***specific states of mind,*** such as calmness, confidence, or aggressiveness, just when you need them.

○ It can help to neutralise the conscious, critical, analytical left-brain part of our thinking that prevents us from doing our best in many situations. ***It harnesses your creative right brain.***

## *Bonus benefits of right-brain visualisation*

As a bonus, it has some big advantages over most physical techniques and training methods.

○ It is ***pleasurable***. Imagining what you want brings pleasure. By creating pleasurable states of mind, the *process* of what you are doing is enjoyable as well as the end result. And it starts before you set foot on the golf course.

○ It is ***convenient***. You don't need to add on travelling time to your practice sessions. You can choose to lie in bed or sit in your favourite armchair.

○ It is ***discreet***. You can fix your goals or do a bit of mental practice when in a boring committee meeting, or in the doctor's waiting room. As you saw in the exercise earlier, you can trigger a confident state of mind without anyone knowing what you are doing.

○ It is *fast*. It is possible to speed up 'your inner movies' and still get benefits. You can easily slot these mental techniques into a normal set-up routine or between holes.

○ It is *positive*. Real life, and golf in particular, is a game full of failures. Misses happen many times more than hits. These mental techniques are the stuff of success.

○ It is *therapeutic*. When you utilise the right brain in this way it is usually associated with relaxation, slower breathing, lower (alpha) brainwaves (explained below), and physical well-being. You can become relaxed on demand, and in the middle of all sorts of external pressure, with appropriate mental imagery. Walter Hagen used to say 'Never hurry. Never worry. Take time to smell the flowers along the way.'

○ It is remarkably *efficient* in terms of the time and effort involved in the process, or the ratio of *effort* to *results*. It gives you *leverage*.

This is such a valuable mental tool that it pays to acquire and develop specific skills. Like physical skills, they may take time to develop, and you need to do it in small steps. So I will describe ways in which you can get the best out of it, starting with mental rehearsal carried out away from the golf course - say when sitting in an armchair or lying in bed before going to sleep.

## *Preparing for mental practice*

The secret of most mental skills is first to get physically relaxed. For many people this is easier said than done. Preparation is important, as you will need some 'quality', uninterrupted time. Although these procedures need not take long, the mind does not seem to like the idea of being interrupted. So if you can get away from the telephone, and somehow arrange to be undisturbed for 20 minutes or so you will find it easier to get into a relaxed state.

Close your eyes and breathe slowly and deeply. If you have used relaxation techniques before, use the technique you find most helpful. There are lots of books specialising in this. You may want to think of each limb as being very heavy, progressively working round your body, so that every part of you, including the neck and shoulders, jaw, and eyelids, is included. Soothing, relaxing music can also help. As you will enter a trance-like state it is useful also to have a simple way of getting back to the external world and getting on with the life you left behind.

Counting downwards, say from 10 to 1, as you become relaxed, will make you associate descending numbers with deeper states of relaxation. Time your countdown session so that you are mentally as well as physically relaxed by the time you get down to 1. Start as high as 50 or 100 if you need to, going down slowly as you imagine each limb getting heavier or whatever system you use. Say the number to yourself or out loud and also see it clearly in your mind. If you wish you can pretend you are writing the number so your visualisation is dynamic and vivid. Or the numbers might appear in computer style as on a big electronic scoreboard. Use your imagination creatively.

# Exercise:
# The 3-2-1 Method of Relaxation

○ Associate the number 3 with complete *physical relaxation.* Initially you may need an extended relaxation session, with a long countdown, to reach a fully relaxed state. But before long you will be able to become relaxed very quickly by the number association, perhaps counting down just from 20, or 10.

○ Associate the number 2 with *mental relaxation,* in which your mind is uncluttered and you have eliminated busy thoughts. In each case repeat and 'see' the number. This level will often be linked with some pleasant visualisation, perhaps a tranquil scene from the past or a fantasy one. So if you have a problem clearing your mind, work on different imaginary scenes that conjure up a pleasant, carefree, tranquil state, perhaps from a childhood memory or a relaxing holiday.

○ Number 1 is then reserved as the *ultimate subjective state* when you can do whatever you want to with the mental techniques we are describing, and make powerful suggestions to your subconscious. This is where you do subjective business, create new realities and fix your outcomes. A few minutes in this productive mental state can be worth hours on the practice ground.

For these final three numbers you should decide on a special representation that you stick to. For example, one might appear in neon lights, in another case you might be writing on a blackboard, or even drawing in the sand on a restful beach. Each of these will then associate with the restful state of mind you are entering. The more bizarre and memorable your visualisation, the more strongly you will anchor your state of mind to the numbers.

## Alpha brain waves

In this state the brain is usually operating at slow alpha waves, rather like the period just before falling asleep, or in a trance-like daydreaming state. You are physically relaxed but your mind is alert and receptive to suggestion. When it comes to installing or changing mental programs or strategies, this is a highly *productive* time. So it pays to become skilled at inducing this alpha state. The more quickly you can do it - and this takes practice - the more readily you will be able to take control of your mind, on and off the golf course.

When you have finished your session, count upwards, and expect to be alert and refreshed as you come out at the count of 10 or, once you are skilled, say at 5. Eventually the process can become a rapid 5 to 1, 1 to 5 technique that will be useful both for 'installing' subjective changes you want to make, and also for getting into a relaxed, empowering state whenever you need to - perhaps just before a match, or an important meeting at work.

You will need this preparatory technique for the mental rehearsal applications later in the chapter, and also for the mental practice described in Chapter 6.

## Getting Into An Empowering State

Having learnt how you can best prepare for mental rehearsal, you are now ready to use it seriously, whether to create inner goals, support beliefs or control how you feel. Use your descending numbers technique to get into a relaxed, alpha state. As you become more familiar with your *subjective* rather than *objective* world, you will get to know yourself better, so that your goals, motivation, beliefs and temperament will be congruent. First your golf then other parts of your life will take on more meaning and be pleasurable. Explore the boundaries of your imagination, and notice how your outlook changes and goals enlarge.

You may find that one modality (seeing, hearing, or feeling), as it is termed, may be more vivid or easier to recall than another, and this just reflects your preference for representing that sense. But spend some time on each of them, as the familiar ones will easily recall the state you want to access, and the less familiar ones might conjure their own useful associations. What you learn will help explain why we are all so different, and will help you to communicate better. This basic mental awareness will also help when you use any of the techniques described later.

## *Exercise:*
## *Creating the Future*

You can use the process for imagining the future as well as drawing on the past. Imagine one of the goals you have set earlier being fulfilled. Make it something you really want to happen, and which will give you a lot of pleasure. What about winning a golf championship? You used the technique earlier to see how easy it is to affect feelings, and when imagining behaviours to support a belief change, but you can now make it part of a serious creative visualisation 'session' and enhance the quality of your visualisation. As with the previous exercise, go through all the sights, sounds and feelings, but this time you can be creative and let your imagination do its own thing. Create the exact outcome you desire. But it need not be any less real than a memory, or for that matter the real thing. The mind is able to *synthesise* realistically drawing on real memories.

Learn to identify the states you enter - maybe give each one a name - tranquillity, confidence, power, determination, mastery, so that you can recall them later, and use them when you need to. You will learn a technique later to do this instantly (see page 117). At the end of a session count back up to 5 and expect to feel wide awake and ready to achieve anything.

## Switching and tweaking submodalities

You can take this a lot further. Each of the three main modalities (seeing, hearing, feeling) has its own characteristics, or submodalities. For example, a visualised scene can be bright or dim, in focus or blurred, in colour or black and white - just as on a television. Similarly, sounds can be loud or soft, with a different pitch or tone. And feelings can be light or heavy, soft or hard etc. Look at Figure 4 on page 116 and you will see just how rich and varied our thought characteristics can be.

Another important way to differentiate a memory or future imagined experience is whether you are seeing things as if through your own eyes (termed associated) or, in effect, watching yourself from outside (termed dissociated). See yourself, for example, as a friend would through a video camera (dissociated), then imagine yourself playing the actual shot, feeling the grip of the club and the ground underfoot. This important distinction can apply in any of the three main representation systems or 'modalities'.

The way you feel, or your state of mind, is formed by all these characteristics together. As you start to recall times when, for instance, you were super confident, although the circumstances or content of your memories may be very different, you may find that these characteristics or submodalities are similar. In other words it is the way we represent things rather than the circumstances themselves that determine how we feel. This opens up big possibilities, because you can change each submodality as you wish, and so change the way you feel about a memory, or something you imagine in the future.

Or, if you wish, you can *intensify* a state of mind - say confidence - by tweaking the submodalities. Usually the brighter, bigger and more lifelike the image, the more impact it makes. So not only can you recall and reuse empowering states, but you can adjust and synthesise them to create just the positive state you need. Neurologically, you can, for instance, become *more* confident.

## VISUAL

| | |
|---|---|
| Brightness | Contrast |
| Size | Clarity |
| Colour/black & wwite | Focus |
| Saturation (vividness) | Framed/panoramic |
| Hue or colour balance | Movement |
| Shape | Perspective |
| Locations | Associated/dissociated |
| Distance | 3-dimensional/flat |

## AUDITORY

| | |
|---|---|
| Pitch | Duration |
| Tempo (speed) | Location |
| Volume | Distance |
| Rhythm | External/internal |
| Continuous/interrupted | Source |
| Timbre or tonality | Mono/stereo |
| Digital (words) | Clarity |
| Associated/dissociated | Number |

## KINAESTHETIC (Sensations)

| | |
|---|---|
| Pressure | Movement |
| Location | Duration |
| Number | Intensity |
| Texture | Shape |
| Temperature | Frequency (tempo) |

**Figure 4** Submodalities Checklist

Check this out. First think of two or three negative memories: choose and name a specific state such as anger, embarrassment, sadness, or whatever, and make a note of all the submodalities. Most golfers have a large memory bank of such emotions. You can use Figure 4 as a checklist. In particular try to spot the main common characteristics, such as whether the imagery is associated or dissociated. Then think of two or three pleasant memories, again choosing and naming a specific state, such as confidence, calmness, optimism and the like. Note all the submodalities associated with these memories. You may find that there are submodalities common to the positive and negative memories respectively.

The same thing happens if you imagine future activities or events. Although you were not thinking of this when you did it, when you thought of different positive and negative outcomes in Chapter 2 the characteristics or submodalities would probably have differed as between the two kinds of thoughts. This explains the different words you used to describe how you felt.

How does this translate into better scores on the golf course? The answer is, by empowering you with the best state of mind to do what you need to. Not only can you recall confidence, but you can also create it. Instead of thinking about an important match with worry and negative feelings, you can imagine the same event but change the characteristics of your thoughts.

## *Exercise:* _____
## *Changing How You Feel*

Instead of shaking with nerves at tee-off or before a critical putt you can feel as calm as you want to be. Here is an exercise that will help you to promote calmness and confidence in different situations.

**1. An important match or round coming up**.   Decide on a state of mind you would like to have for a forthcoming event or activity you are worried or anxious about. From the exercise you have just done identify the submodalities which for you are associated with that state of mind. If you need to, choose other memories that accurately reflect the state you want to repeat. Use the submodalities check list if you need to. Now replace, one by one, each submodality of the imagined activity with empowering ones you have identified. For example, if your negative images are small and out of focus, but your positive images are big and bright, then make everything big and bright. Or if your disempowering images are dissociated (you see yourself as from the outside), but your positive memories were associated (you saw as if through your own eyes, and experienced how you felt), then make sure you become associated. Go through sights, sounds and feelings separately, then together, incorporating all your changed submodalities.

You will probably now feel differently about what were previously anxious, unpleasant thoughts - to be precise, you will feel as you did on the happy occasions you recalled. Then by repeated visualisation of the activity or event you are preparing for, you will not only associate it with good feelings, but you will give yourself practice, so that the real thing seems familiar rather than unknown and threatening. This is what gives you confidence.

**2.  A shot, hole, or course you are unhappy about**. There may be a particular kind of shot you feel unhappy about. So use the same process. Recall an occasion when you played the shot well, and felt really good. If need be, improve any aspect of the shot until you are entirely happy with it, first dissociated, then step inside yourself and become associated. Check the submodalities in as much detail as possible, again referring to your check list if you need to.  Note all the sights, sounds and feelings, both external (what you actually saw, the feel of the ground underfoot, your grip, the sound of the club going through the air) and internal (images inside such as the target, words that went through your mind, or a feeling in the pit of your stomach). Think about the moments *before* you played the shot as well as when you were executing it.

Now imagine you are doing the shot next week or some time in the future, but switch all the empowering submodalities to replace the disempowering ones. You will then create the feeling you had, and that you want to have every time you make the shot. If you need to, you can also change the main modalities - that is you can look at, listen to and feel different things - as well as representing them in a different way. In fact the exercise is likely to identify the crucial difference between when you make a good shot and a bad one. This is the *difference that makes the difference*, which is your key to excellence. Use this process for a particular hole that has had negative associations, or a course that you are not happy playing on. If you do not have any success memories of the specific hole or course then 'borrow' them from another. It is the state of mind you are recalling and harnessing.

**3. Winning**.   You want to succeed in winning awards or some accolade, but you have identified 'ecology' that is not right. For instance, you may be unhappy about the public attention, having to give a speech, the pressure you will have to face next time, or some other change in your life. You may not initially be aware of these ecological factors, but they should become apparent from outcome tests in Chapter 2. You can now allow for these, by drawing on occasions when you enjoyed the state of mind you wish for, and switching the submodalities just as you did in the previous two cases. In this case you may have to draw on memories outside your golf - most of us perform differently in different parts of our life, such as work, family, social etc., so you can draw on your own mastery in any area you like. Your thought characteristics, or submodalities, are common to all these situations. You just have to identify them and use them where you need to.

Billy Casper was never afraid of money tournaments, but when it came to titles, and the important ones, something seemed to ebb from his determination. We each have our own mental hang-ups, about winning, losing and the associations we have with particular outcomes. Mental techniques rather than further swing analysis come to our rescue in these situations.

## Future testing

After a suitable interval, when you have been doing other things, you can check out whether you feel differently now about the thing you were anxious about. Repeat the process if you need to until you instinctively feel good about whatever was bothering you. By using this technique you can be prepared for anything you have to face.

In a similar way you can also *test out* a future scenario you are unsure about, and get a good idea of whether it is right for you, and what the downsides might be. For example, you can imagine what it would be like to be a professional, playing off scratch, or winning an important tournament. This will be an opportunity to experience some of the pleasures and pitfalls of the game at a higher level - you can do all this with your limitless imagination.

One seminar delegate did a 'future pace' on a dream holiday he had always wished for, only to find that he got bored after three or four days and decided it was not really what he wanted! He got that particular dream out of his system, saving himself a lot of disappointment and money into the bargain. A 3-handicapper did some future pacing about turning professional and found that he was not mentally prepared for it, even though he had the talent. In his case this explained why he had been stuck at his handicap level for a long time. In fact his unconscious was protecting him from something that was perceived as harmful or frightening. Having identified the situation, he was free to decide about the 'ecology'. Having sorted out his outcomes better, he could again test them out by future pacing.

Any major change involving golf or another aspect of your life might benefit from the same right-brain, forward looking thought. You now have a technique you can use to change the state you are in. You can also use the technique to try out any outcome. Any goal is strengthened by this internal test, and its chances of success are multiplied.

## Anchoring

An anchor is either an internal or external sight, sound, or other sensation that triggers a past experience in the memory. A tune, an old photograph, or even a smell can quickly take you back to experience even a distant memory. An old trusty golf club can have a beneficial anchoring effect, while the sight of the lake in which you lost the ball the other week can anchor the wrong emotions. As well as recalling the sights and sounds, you also recall the feelings associated, so your state of mind can change instantly if an appropriate anchor stimulates it. A phobia is a good example of an anchor, in which a trigger, such as the sight of a spider or the sound of an aircraft engine, can instantly and consistently capture an extreme emotion. If you have any sort of phobia you have already perfected the technique of anchoring which you can now use positively. Our lives are full of anchors, some of which are positive, triggering pleasant or useful emotions, and some negative, which we could well do without. By creating appropriate anchors you can use this common, powerful mental phenomenon to your advantage, and get into the state of mind you want quickly.

## Resource anchoring

How can you anchor any chosen mental resource, such as confidence, calmness, or competitiveness? First, here is a word about the anchors you will be creating. A *kinaesthetic* anchor is a physical action or gesture you can easily and discreetly carry out. For instance you can apply finger pressure against a specific part of your body, touch your thumb with your fourth finger, crunch up your right toes, or whatever. Just make sure that the anchor is unique to the particular state you want to recall. A *visual* anchor is an inner or outer picture of something you associate with the resource. You might, for instance, visualise a scene from a time you made the shot in question superbly, or any scene or object that you link with the confidence, calmness or whatever state you want. An *auditory* anchor is a sound, or something you say to yourself - perhaps a positive phrase that helps you, or even a favourite tune.

Here is a simple anchoring process:

1. Identify the resource you need to accomplish a particular outcome or execute a particular shot.

2. Remember an occasion when you had that resource, and used it successfully.

3. Relive the experience, vividly recalling all the sights, sounds and feelings.

4. Intensify all the emotions, leading up to and during the activity. Anchor your emotional feelings with finger pressure, and also a sound and image as described above.

5. Practise 'firing' the anchor several times a day until you can immediately capture the resource you need.

## Contextualising your anchor

If you need the resource in question every time you carry out a particular shot, or activity, it may help if you build it into your normal pre-shot routine, or teeing off etc. routine. In this case the finger pressure could, for instance, be linked to your grip. Visual and auditory images can be applied internally, as in the exercise, but you may want to use external anchors that are also part of your routine. For example, you can look at a spot on the ball, your left foot, or whatever, as an external pre-shot visual anchor. Similarly, you could look at the tee marker as a visual anchor for a teeing off resource. If you just want the resource on certain occasions, say when you want more determination, you can still contextualise your anchor, say by tying your shoelaces, or wiping your club clean. This is added to your pre-shot routine in those circumstances.

## Automatic anchors

To convert a simple finger pressure anchor into an external contextualised one, just practise them together for a while, so that one is always associated with the other. By simply thinking about the external anchors when you establish the finger pressure anchor you will be able to get the association, then you can reinforce it on practice rounds. Soon you will only need the routine anchors, which of course become automatic as you establish the habits. The idea in any case is to make your anchors work automatically, just as they do in everyday life, such as when you see a red traffic signal, or hear the alarm clock in the morning.

## Your anchor portfolio

You can establish an anchor for each resource you need. The only requirement is to recall a memory - any memory - in which you had the resource you want to have on call. And even here you can manipulate and intensify the resource by using the submodality switching described above. Make sure that each anchor, whether internal or external, is unique to the resource state you want, so that is the *only* association between the anchor and the state.

## Empowering states to anchor

Use this technique to anchor the following states:

○ Confidence.

○ Optimism.

○ Calmness.

○ Patience.

○ Determination.

○ Competitiveness.

○ Concentration.

○ Carefreeness.

○ Self-esteem.

○ Persistence.

Or recall specific empowering states you cannot give a name to ('If only I could feel the way I felt last year at Collingtree when I made that string of birdies'), but want to recapture at will.

## Applying your anchors

You can then apply your resource anchors in the following specific situations:

○ Teeing off.

○ Specific problem shots.

○ Shots critical to your score and results.

○ Following double bogies, penalties or freak shots.

○ Poor greens.

○ Annoying partners.

○ The half-hour before the start of a tournament.

○ Slow players ahead of you.

○ Running late for a game.

○ Weather you don't like.

Or you can apply them to any situation which for you triggers the wrong emotional state.

You now have techniques to change the way you feel, either to plan for a particular event or circumstance, or to be ready to quickly trigger a state whenever you need it - a portfolio of resource anchors to meet any situation. You should now be able to eliminate a lot of problem shots and circumstances which are tied up with your state of mind, and start to get the control upon which consistency depends.

## Masterstroke Question Clinic

**1. *How can I stop shaking with fear on the first tee?***
Use the techniques just described, including mental preparation a few hours before. Also make sure you have a consistent set-up routine which you stick to.

**2. *I feel so depressed when I play badly. What can I do?***
Try to identify the shots, holes, courses, or particular circumstances that are associated with your bad feelings. Has there ever been a time you played badly but did *not* feel depressed? Use the above process, applying it to as many specific depressing situations as you can think of. Go back

to your hierarchy of goals, and try to get your golf in perspective. After all, if you miss a 3-ft putt it doesn't mean you are a bad parent or no good at your job. Pay particular attention to the ecology check, in the tests of a well-formed outcome (Chapter 2). Check also whether any of the self-beliefs you identified support this kind of feeling, and use the belief change process to change your disempowering belief.

### 3. I always seem to make a mess of the sixth hole at my home course. Why?

You may be able to recall a horror shot which has stayed with you, but it doesn't matter if you can't find a reason. The main thing is to correct it, and you can do this by using the Changing How You Feel technique (variation 2) you learnt (page 117).

### 4. I get so annoyed, sometimes I feel like breaking my clubs. Why do I get so upset?

First think about perspective on the game, as I said in answer to question 2. Then use the anchoring technique to call up the calmness you need just when you need it. You may be able to identify situations when this is most likely to occur - for instance a particular shot, or when the green is in poor condition. Then apply the state change technique to the particular shot or situation. Work on your self-beliefs (Chapter 3). The sun will come up tomorrow whatever score you get.

### 5. Under pressure I seem to rush everything, then my game goes. Why?

There could be many reasons but I assume you want to put the situation right. Decide on a more appropriate state and use the techniques you have learnt to change. If you know a pressure situation is coming up, say in a competitive match, you can prepare for it. Have a look at Chapter 5 which covers rhythm, and also at Chapter 6 on practice. If it just seems to occur out of the blue get your state anchored (above), so that you can apply it instantly. In effect you can remove yourself to a place where you feel no pressure. Remember also the importance of a solid pre-stroke routine. A familiar routine, and a clear target (look back at Chapter 2) will fill your conscious mind, so there is no room for pressure thoughts. Pressure doesn't exist in the way that rain or poor greens do - we create it; it's entirely subjective. With that understanding it is not hard to believe we can uncreate it.

### 6. *We have terrible greens on our course and I always putt badly. What do I do?*

You have learnt that your attitude is something you can control, and the Changing How You Feel technique (variation 2) works well with specific situations like this. Remember that if you are to get anywhere in the game you have to accept greens as you find them. All your competitors are in the same boat. Some players are particularly good in wind, rain, or on poor greens, because they have gained their experience that way and have developed the right attitude.

### 7. *When I really want to impress someone I usually play badly. How can I overcome this?*

Decide on your own goals so you only have yourself to also impress. And look back also at goals in Chapter 2 to see how you can maintain shot by shot focus, which will fully occupy your mind.

## 8. I never play well in the rain. Why is this?

This is a classic self-fulfilling negative self-belief of the sort we met in Chapter 3. You have learnt this particular response well, so you are quite able to learn new ones that serve you better. Use the belief change technique to do this, or the above mental rehearsal techniques just as you would for a problem shot, or course. Have you ever played a good shot in the rain? Then you have the basis to 'anchor' the rain to your advantage.

## 9. Do good players get annoyed at bad shots?

Yes, but they don't let it affect their game. It's OK to get annoyed from time to time. It's not OK to let one or two rogue shots ruin your game. And there is a difference between being angry at a bad shot and being angry with yourself. Use the state control techniques we have described to depersonalise or channel your anger.

## 10. Does equipment make any difference?

Sure, if you believe it does. But based on vast anecdotal evidence, it's the mental side of the game that tips the balance when it comes to scores.

## 11. I feel very self-conscious on a golf course. I am scared stiff of making a mistake in front of my husband. What do I do?

Use the techniques in this chapter to give you control over how you feel at these times. You may also have identified a negative self-belief that is linked to this situation, in which case you can also create more empowering ones as you learnt in Chapter 3.

## 12. If the pace of play gets too slow I play terribly. Why?

This is also about your state of mind. It could also be that slow play gives you more time to think analytically or critically rather than playing spontaneously. In any event use your time wisely with thoughts that you decide will help rather than hinder. You can use the time between holes to repeat your empowering images - this is valuable mental practice time.

## 13. Under real pressure in a tournament how can I stay in control?

Look above at preparing for a big event like this, as well as shot by shot control and a consistent pre-shot routine which is the basis of handling pressure. Do you know how it will feel if you win? Check it out by future pacing (testing), as this may test out goals and self-beliefs that affect the situation. Expect a healthy level of pressure, of course - that's part of the 'system's' way of motivating and goal-achieving. But note what the answer to question 5 says about what pressure is.

## 14. I feel physically shattered after a round of golf yet I am very fit. Why?

It sounds as though you are too intense. Think about your target and results (outputs) rather than the effort you put in (inputs). Work on the relaxation exercises and look on the walk between holes as a chance for physical and mental relaxation. Don't spoil a good walk and the joys of nature with golf!

## 15. Why do I shake over a 3-ft putt?

The memory of previous horror putts? The fear of

failure? Or if it is a critical final hole putt - the fear of success? Bernard Langer knows something about the 'yips' when putting, so don't be too hard on yourself. Try the state control techniques above and check on your goal priorities and beliefs, about yourself and short putts (previous two chapters). You will also pick up some useful tips for your short game in Chapter 6 on practice.

### 16. My arms feel really tight when I address the ball. What can I do?

Practise extended relaxation, but, more importantly, the technique of anchoring your relaxed state. Practise switching on your state any time, anywhere, so that it is natural and even automatic. Build in relaxation anchors to your normal set-up routine, so you don't even have to 'remember' to do it. You should find the modelling techniques in Chapter 5 helpful, as you can draw specifically on whoever you think has a relaxed address position.

# 5 ▷ MODELLING A PERFECT SWING

**N**O *TWO* players can possibly swing the club the same way, although that is what the swing doctors are trying to achieve. The differences are due to our physical and mental make-up. Your swing is unique to you, although subject to certain 'basics', and, as we shall see in this chapter, in learning mode you can model your swing on anyone you like.

You should now have a good mental foundation on which you can build a sound swing, any shot, and an ongoing improvement in scores. You know the principles that can be applied to your goals at every level in the game, and your beliefs should now be supportive of whatever you learn and attempt, and your attitude positive.

Some fundamental aspects of the game don't need a golf course to learn them, like holding and swinging the club to hit the ball solid. These are so basic that you can hardly embark on a 'game' as such without getting them reasonably right, whatever your confidence level or self-image. In

the long run it really pays to get the fundamentals sound
and habitual, and this particularly applies to your swing,
hold (grip) and set-up. So in this chapter we will discuss
these fundamentals in some depth, from the point of view
of *learning* how to do them rather than just knowing about
them, or analysing them. You will learn how to learn, using
the modelling methods we discussed in the first chapter.
We want to emphasise again that golf is not *just* mental, any
more than it is just physical. To do well in the game you
need to have a sound mechanically repeating swing allied to
a mental state that allows you to use it consistently to your
maximum potential.

You have already learnt the power of visualising a goal,
and seeing yourself as you want to be. But every such vision
or dream is subject to getting certain fundamentals right -
there is no short cut in that sense. And your visualisation
has also to conform with the natural laws of force and
motion. Whatever goes on in your mind, if your golf swing
does not result in you hitting the ball squarely in the
direction it has to go, you will miss your target and never
achieve much in golf. Until you have grasped these
fundamentals, a more sensible use of visualisation is to
reinforce the belief that you can *learn* to become a great
golfer. *See yourself* grasping or perfecting the fundamentals.
The various skills needed to master these basics become
separate, interim learning goals on your journey towards
consistency and excellence. These fundamental skills are
not golf, but you can't play golf without them.

You will use the four-part masterstroke model as you
tackle each learning objective:

1. Decide what you want (say, to have a sound basic grip, or
   address position).

2. Do what is suggested in the exercises that follow.

3. Notice exactly what happens.

4. Have another go, slightly changing what you do to achieve a better result.

In particular be prepared to repeat the learning cycle as many times as it takes to form a *habit* of each basic activity. Once you have formed the habit, the cybernetic (automatic goal-seeking) programme is installed, and you can trust the system. You don't interfere unless you have a major, fundamental weakness. Your conscious learning is then switched to other aspects of the game, like making shots and scores. Get these foundations right and it will repay the effort for a whole lifetime of pleasure in the game.

In this chapter we describe a method of learning the main components of the swing in a way that optimises your whole brain - the right side as well as the left. It incorporates the sort of vivid visualisation you have already met, but this is now directed to specific *learning* goals, rather than score and handicap goals, or states of mind. It also incorporates the powerful principles of modelling behaviour, upon which NLP is based. The main difference between this method and what you may have done before is not so much the information, but how that information is processed in your mind. As it happens, there is extraordinary agreement among top players about the *fundamentals* of the hold and set-up, and to a lesser degree the swing itself. After all, much of it is just complying mechanically with well-known natural laws. But every professional teacher has a different method of getting this information across, and every half-serious golfer becomes a self-appointed teacher, adviser, or even expert before long. Unfortunately, we all get too clever by half and forget what natural learning is all about.

## Imitating Excellence

The idea of imitating, or modelling, is not new. Bobby Jones lived in a house near the 13th hole of the Atlanta Athletic Club, and learnt the game from a Scottish pro named Stewart Maiden. Jones would tag along behind Maiden imitating his movements. Like Jones, Walter Hagen learnt his swing by imitating, though he did it as a caddie. Another caddie turned golf teacher (a 'grown up caddie' as he called himself), Harvey Penick, learned to imitate the swing of every player in the club and for a nickel or a dime would put on a show. Imitation, or modelling, is central to human learning. With developments in neuro-linguistic programming, this modelling process is now better understood. What the great players of the past did without understanding how it worked can be learnt by anyone, and used in a more deliberate, predictable way.

Young children give us a classic example of how we can learn quickly and effectively, with enjoyment into the bargain. Although we rarely, as adults, fully regain that childlike uninhibited mode of learning, we can certainly draw on the learning system that is being used. Not surprisingly, being so effective in the case of children, it is disarmingly *simple*. Sure, hundreds of muscle movements and chemical happenings in the brain and body take place but the same might be the case when you make a cup of tea or chase a cat out of the garden (try and get a robot to do either). As far as your *conscious* mind is concerned, any complex activity can be learnt simply - if necessary, like driving a car, or making a soufflé, one little step at a time. And once learnt, you can do these things *without thinking*, so they *remain* simple, whatever level of expertise you rise to. If you think about what your legs are doing every time you negotiate the stairs you are likely to break a leg. In this category of 'automatic' skills lies the infamous golf swing, however it has been elevated, analysed and mystified by experts and critics.

The technique you will use is ideal for the golf swing, but can be applied to learning any activity or skill. As it is based on human 'models', you need to be able to watch, either in person or on the television or video, golfers who have mastered the basics you want to learn. So it will obviously help if you have the use of a video player, although that is not essential. The various steps in the process will be applied to each of the key components of your swing and swing preparation:

○ Holding the club.

○ Set position (address, posture and alignment).

○ Starting the swing.

○ Power generation.

○ Club positioning.

○ Impact alignments.

○ Rhythm.

○ Putting it all together.

Here are the steps:

## *Step 1*

Choose a model who performs perfectly the action you want to copy. Any competent model will do, such as your club professional or a colleague whom you particularly admire as regards the specific activity in question. But, at this stage in your learning at least, you will never be better than your model, so go for the best. Henry Cotton advised all young players: 'Watch only the best players. See what they do that makes them different. Then pinch it. But never try to make yourself a direct copy of any other man. You have your own talent. You are your own man.' So you are in good company with the modelling technique, and you have second-to-none testimony to its effectiveness.

Your model, however, need not be a super all-rounder, but rather needs to be effective in the component (above) or aspect of the swing you want to emulate. This allows you to go for excellence. The closer you can observe, then imitate the model, the better you will be able to use this technique.

## Step 2

Watch the model performing the activity as many times as possible, from as many angles as you can. Concentrate on the positioning, the movements, the pace, the flow. Whenever you think of the activity in question, this image should come to your mind, just as a favourite song can instantly recall a distant memory.

## Step 3

Now turn the model into yourself - see your own face on the person, as *you* now carry out the activity perfectly. You are still dissociated, however, watching the action from outside, even though it is yourself you are now watching.

## Step 4

Now step into the picture and see things through your own eyes, and feel things through your own body. Become your model. Keep repeating the activity until it is a natural part of you, just like climbing up stairs or cleaning your teeth. Make any adjustments you need to until you have completely mastered the activity. Having done the exercise mentally, you can easily start performing the skill physically, checking in a mirror or with a video recording that you have 'become' your model. You don't need to practise with balls at this stage, or on a golf course, but you do need to get accurate feedback about what you are doing.

## Role-play

That's the procedure for each component of the swing. This technique involves imitation, but also some role-playing. In other words, as well as copying what your model *does*, you *become* the person, so you will think and behave, including mannerisms, pace and temperament, like your model. Children take to role-playing easily and in a competitive game one might become Faldo and the other Seve, mimicking every aspect of their heroes as well as quickly adopting their respective swings. Adults are much more inhibited, although club players often find their game strangely goes up a notch or two after watching top players on television. All of us were young at one time, with childlike imaginations, so it is more a matter of rekindling a latent mental skill than learning something completely new. Perhaps in your dream or private world you do imagine yourself to be a great golfer; that's fine, but this technique involves using this inbuilt creative ability in a positive, directed way, rather than as part of an unstructured dream life.

## Relaxing and the alpha state

For these exercises you will need to get into a relaxed, alpha state as you learnt in Chapter 4, and find a quiet place and time of the day when you are not likely to be interrupted. Initially you might have difficulty focusing in a non-analytical way, but the more you do it the easier it will become, and into the bargain it is very enjoyable and therapeutic. As well as physical relaxation, the slow alpha state is linked with a mental calmness, when your mind, although alert, is emptied of 'busy' thoughts. The 3-2-1 process will help to enter the receptive state you need. Don't listen to your inner critical self that might tell you you could be doing something more worth while, or giving clever advice on some minute aspect of what you are doing.

Apply the four steps to each aspect of your overall swing as numbered below. The swing is one movement, of course, but for learning purposes you should just take in what you are able. Just as when learning to drive a car, lesson by lesson you concentrate on different aspects such as steering, rear mirror, changing gear, etc., so in these exercises you will learn the fundamentals in chunks. Another reason why we have broken down the overall swing in this way is that you will be able to experience drawing on different models who have different strengths. You can later use the same technique to model any total swing you care to choose.

That is all there is to it, but we will comment on each aspect of the overall swing so that you will not just become familiar with the process, but will also be able to carry it out on a do-it-yourself basis. For the moment, keep to the order we have used, although in practice, as you will see later, you will be able to model the total swing as well as aspects of it.

## 1. *Holding the club* _____
*Suggested models* Nick Faldo, Severiano Ballesteros

If there is one absolutely mandatory technical fundamental it is the correct hold on the club. Byron Nelson says: 'The grip is the most important consideration in learning to play winning golf'. And the great Bobby Jones is on record as remarking: 'A correct grip is a fundamental necessity in the golf swing'. Note I have called it a hold and not a grip. Grip has all the wrong connotations, linked as it is with pressure and tension, although that is the term generally in use, and we have used it elsewhere in the book, mainly in quotations.

How you place your hands on the club is important. The importance is summarised by the simple equation 'Hands = club face'. The way you arrange your hands on the club will directly affect the face of the club and in turn the flight of the ball. However perfect your swing, there is no short cut here, so it is worth the time and effort in getting it right. Having said this, there is no mystery - you just have to follow simple rules and apply the modelling principles.

In this case you will need to get some good close-up pictures. This is where your mental camera will have to zoom in. As with the other parts of the swing, it is fine if you have access to a real life model, or a professional who has the patience to take you through the process at your speed. Alternatively, there are many excellent magazine photographs of top players, or specialised videos, which will serve the same purpose.

Figures 5a to 5g show you the sequence, and the important features to watch out for in your model. Use only a light pressure - like a gentle handshake, or handling a delicate musical instrument - rather than strangling the club. The pressure of the grip has been likened to holding a live bird - just enough so the bird can breathe, but can't fly away.

### Figure 5a
Hold the club shaft up in the air in your right hand with the leading edge of the face pointing straight to the sky.

### Figure 5b
Bring your left hand in from the side (not underneath) and place the club diagonally across your palm so that it runs through the palm into the fingers - not all palm. The club runs from the middle joint of your left index finger to just under the base of your little finger.

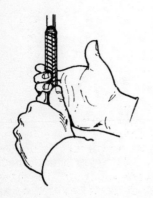

### Figure 5c
You will also find that your left thumb sits slightly to the right of the grip with no gap between the thumb and forefinger.

### Figure 5d

Now simply slide your right hand down the club which is being held primarily in the fingers until the two hands meet. The hands should fit snugly together with the fleshy part of the right hand over the thumb of the left hand. Your right thumb will be slightly to the left side of the shaft.

### Figure 5e

You can join your hands by simply overlapping the index finger of your right hand between the middle and first fingers of the left hand.

### Figure 5f

Or simply let the hands sit together in what is known as the ten finger or baseball grip. This is especially useful for the woman golfer with small to average size hands, and the junior golfer.

### Figure 5g

Looking from the front the overall picture is one of the hands being a unit that will work together. The hands should feel as if they are melted together.

## 2. *The set position*_____
*Suggested models*  Lee Janzen, Nick Faldo

Most mistakes are made before the club is swung. Get hold of still or video pictures of the model of your choice in the set or 'address' position. It helps if you can view your model from as many angles as possible, so you will appreciate the advantage of having a live model to watch, and also the benefit of a comprehensive video recording over a still photograph. Just trust your brain to absorb every aspect of your model - even parts of the operation that you are not conscious of. This simple trust will speed up your learning, which will also have a longer lasting effect.

Follow each step, first seeing your model vividly from different angles, then becoming the model by seeing yourself (dissociated), and finally stepping inside to become fully associated. Do this as many times as you need to. The whole process need not take long, as your mind can carry out lots of rehearsals in a short space of time. With each repetition, fine-tune your performance so that it gets progressively nearer to perfection. This process follows the four-part masterstroke model (see page 27), in which you use sensory acuity and are flexible to change until you can consistently 'hit' your visualisation target. Your goal, in each case, is to master that particular skill.

In your associated mode you will soon 'feel' the perfect set position. The straight back tilted from the hips to allow your arms to swing; your weight evenly distributed between both feet; the sense of balance and poise. Shoulders, hips and feet should be parallel to the target. Get to know and enjoy these experiences, which will soon become instinctive and consistent. *Sense* your progress rather than analysing it. Trust your eyes and feelings as you see your model, then yourself in the mirror. Don't allow your head to become full of words and instructions. These intricate skills can hardly be described in language. The process is easy and natural. You did it all the time when you were a child, learning quickly and effectively hundreds of new skills that have stayed with you for life, without an instruction book or professional trainer in sight. This is normal human learning, for which you are purposely designed, at its awesome best. So tap into it.

**Figure 5h**
The Set Position
(at address)

## 3. Starting the swing _____

*Suggested models* Greg Norman, Ernie Els, Tom Kite

Follow the same process for the start of the swing. Start from a relaxed position. Creating smooth, rhythmic movement from a tense position is just about impossible. Note what your model does immediately before starting to swing. Allow your shoulders, arms and hands to feel 'soft'. The models we have suggested start the swing with a one-piece movement of the arms and shoulders away from the ball - there is no jerky pickup with the hands only. If the initial moments of the swing are right, there is every chance that the rest of it will be sound. You can test it by making lots of practice swings without a ball, so ingraining the feeling. But your fundamental learning will come about simply by following the four-step procedure. You will *notice* these features, and others, as you carefully watch, copy and feel.

**Figure 5i**
Starting
the Swing

## 4. *Power generation*
*Suggested models* John Daly, Laura Davis, Ian Woosnam

As you watch your model you will be reminded of a spring coil winding and unwinding. The whole body is the spring, rather than just the hands and arms. In fact, this is the only way that the enormous force needed can be applied to the ball to generate the kind of speeds that carry the great distances required. Hitting and lungeing at the ball - however fiercely - will simply not generate the power needed. See how the upper body seems to wind up against the resistance of the lower body. Note how the knees hold very still in the backswing creating the torque action. All this torque is then released through the downswing, transferring all the power out through the arms and into the club head. It is this coiling and uncoiling motion that makes a good swing look effortless, even though the ball is sent enormous distances. There is little or no physical *effort*.

The phenomenon has been described in many ways. Bobby Jones, for example, is quoted as saying: 'Trial and experiment demonstrated to me that the necessary whirling motion of the club was produced only when the force activating the club had its origins in the centre of the body'. This will become more apparent as you soak up your model and experience it for yourself. It is then just a little step further to experience the whole swing, the start, backswing and downswing, as a single, smooth, rhythmic operation.

**Figure 5j**
Power Generation

## 5. *Club positioning* _____

*Suggested models*  Nick Faldo, Mark O'Meara

It's no use creating club head speed if you have no control over where the speed is being directed. Some very basic natural laws operate, and you have to apply pressure to the golf ball at the correct angle. And you don't need to have a mathematics degree to work out that the tiniest difference in the angle you hit the ball will be multiplied as it careers through the sky. No such standards of accuracy apply in tennis, soccer and most other ball games. So these fundamentals, most of which you can learn before you ever step on to a golf course, are really important. As well as the need for amazing levels of accuracy, which require the correct technique, properly learnt fundamentals will mean you start off with good habits rather than bad ones which, sooner or later, have to be unlearned.

We have treated this separately from the previous two parts of the swing so that you can concentrate only on the physical movements of your model without having to think also about what is happening to the club and club head in particular. But as a separate modelling exercise you will be able to get this part of it right just as naturally.

In this case make sure you see your model from the rear. From this viewing position you will pick up three important check point positions. Your mini goal for this part of the operation is to swing the club through the correct plane. If you do this and the club face hits the ball at the right angle you will make consistently good shots. The check is simple - you are either on the right plane or you are not. The first check point is when the club is parallel to the ground on the moveaway. If the club is on plane at this point, the shaft will be parallel to the direction of your intended shot (Figure

5k). At the top of the swing the club is again parallel to your target (Figure 5l). Then on into the downswing your approach to impact should be a mirror image of your takeaway.

**Figure 5k**
Shaft parallel
to target

**Figure 5l**
Club parallel
to target

As well as the club being on plane the club face needs also to be under control. The check points for the club face are:

○ When the club is parallel to the ground the leading edge of the club face should point directly to the sky.

○ At the top of the backswing the club face hangs at an angle of 45 degrees. If the club face points to the sky, this position is termed closed. If the toe of the club points directly to the ground, this is an open face.

Either position would need some compensation on the downswing, so would lead to an inconsistent swing. On the downswing when the club is parallel to the ground, the club position is that of the leading edge pointing to the sky.

These checks are just to help you notice more about what your model is doing in a very specific aspect of the swing. It will help your sensory acuity. But the process of learning remains the same - watch, copy, and adjust until you become just the same as your model. In this case you will need to do the simple checks from a dissociated viewpoint, so that you can always see what the club head is doing. Once you are happy with this, you can get *inside* your model and feel what it is like to have the perfect club alignment all the way through. Although you cannot see the club head, you should become aware of its precise position in space and its angle in relation to the ground and the sky. This is what control is all about, and although it involves fantastic physical skills, it all starts in the mind. Once again, club positioning will become part of a single, rhythmic, swing motion.

## 6. Impact alignments

*Suggested models* Ben Hogan, Nick Price

Now comes the moment of truth. The only position that your golf ball cares about is how the club face actually hits it. The whole swing is about making this connection accurately and consistently. It lasts for a fraction of a second. There is impact, then the club face and ball separate. During this minute period of time the ball compresses, then springs ballistically off the club face, while the club shaft bends and springs back in the same moments. And the operation is not over until it is over, although most golfers' swings collapse before the ball finally separates from the club face.

By the time you feel this impact, the ball has already left the club face - it happens so fast. So you need to picture and feel this final part of your swing just before it happens in order to tune your system, and thus allow the necessary alignments to be carried out unconsciously.

If you look at your model closely you will see that at impact the club shaft is leaning slightly, a little behind the angle of your arm. At separation, however, the left arm and club are in line. From the back, you will see that the body is not in the same position as it was at address. It is slightly open at the hips. The impression you will get from watching great golfers is that they are *pressing* the ball up into the air, rather than trying to flick it up. Great players have talked about the feeling that the ball and club seem to be together for a long time at impact when they are playing their best golf, using terms like 'heavy' to describe the sensation of the club meeting the ball.

As you work through this modelling exercise you will develop your own appropriate sensations. These are part of your perfect, consistent swing. They will become familiar, and you will come to depend upon them. You will associate good shots with certain feelings, mental images, or perhaps sounds. And because you can recall, or replicate those images, you can bring mastery and consistency to your swing. Although you can adjust any aspect of your golf by using this same process - in other words it is possible to remodel any behaviour - just like learning to swim or ride a bike, the essentials seem to stay with you. So get it right, and it will stay right.

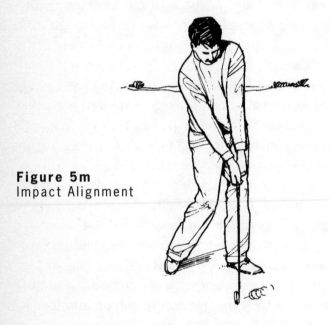

**Figure 5m**
Impact Alignment

# 7. *Rhythm*

*Suggested models* Fred Couples, Ian Woosnam

This is the final, and perhaps most important component of a sound swing. No matter how accurately you may position your club, if your timing is off you will not produce your best. Many great players do not have a technically perfect swing, but they have the important strength of rhythm and make in-swing compensation that produces the results. This is how Mike Hebron, top US coach, put it: 'Stay smooth when you play golf. Take your time, relax and play "in the state of grace". Your golf swing does not have to be fast or hard to have power.'

Tension is the big enemy of rhythm. When your muscles are tight and tense it is nigh on impossible to swing your club at the correct pace. Rhythm, incidentally, does not mean slow, if that is the impression you have got from the magazines. Nick Price and Tom Watson both have rhythmic swings that could never be described as slow. Rhythm is swinging the club at the pace that maintains full control, and is right for you. It is a very personal thing, and it might well reflect other aspects of your personality. A person who talks, drives and eats quickly might well have a swing to match, for instance, and conversely a more deliberate person will have a similarly matching swing. So let your swing fit your personality. You may have to choose models that you relate to in style and temperament, as well as for their technical excellence.

One of the sayings of Confucius, although not perhaps in the context of his golf swing, is: 'It does not matter how slowly you go as long as you don't stop.' Rhythm, or timing, is often associated with music, of course, and it might be useful to imagine the tune that would best fit your model's swing. As you soak up their swing you can play the tune in your head and so match their rhythm. As in many other sports, you are aiming for grace, balance and economy of effort. Each of your main senses - seeing, hearing and feeling - can be harnessed into achieving these excellent characteristics.

Go through the pictures, or video of your models over and over until you can feel as well as easily visualise each step. As you progress to using an actual club you can start exploring how the positions feel. You will soon be familiar with all the tactile sensations of exactly where to place your hands.

Don't rely on any word description of this important fundamental. The above narrative is simply for you to relate what you see in your photographs, video or live model as a sequence so that each stage can be easily learnt. Even though this stage does not call on the same hundreds of muscles as the downswing, the learning process is the same, and you are storing up a tactile memory blueprint that will serve you well for many years.

Don't forget what you have already learnt. Everything so far is still valid. Remember in particular the four-part masterstroke model. This is another example in operation.

○ Decide you are going to learn a dependable hold, set position, etc. that will be the basis for the highest level of accuracy in your swing (your learning goal).

○ Have a go - try it.

○ Notice what it looks, sounds and feels like, and check against your model. Practise your sensory acuity skills.

○ Make any adjustment you have to until you perfectly model, and have the confidence to repeat, the process again and again. Be flexible. Using this process you can only get nearer your learning goal. You can't fail; you can only learn.

Repeat the cycle. Form habits - good habits based on sound fundamental skills. Don't be slow to copy others, and while you are doing so you may as well choose the best models around.

## Putting It All Together

Now you have got the fundamentals, you can put it all together. The swing, of course, is one activity. It doesn't break down well into parts any more than a great poem can be analysed into words. I have broken it down into a few key aspects so that each learning goal is manageable - the chunks are not too big to take in - and also so that you can choose models who excel in those aspects of the swing. You can thus draw on the very best. What remains, however, is to adopt a swing - and you can use the same modelling principles - that is a single, flowing, rhythmic movement. It is one operation rather than several. In golf, as in other sports, the whole is greater than the sum of the parts. So this stage is especially important. Essentially, having learnt the fundamentals, you have to stop learning. In fact stop thinking, and *just do it*. If you have followed the above process you will have the inner blueprint of a sound, repeating golf swing. This is the time to stop training and start trusting.

### *Analysis paralysis*

Here's how Severiano Ballesteros describes his feelings:

> Once I feel ready to go, I trigger the backswing by gently pulling the club away from the ball with my right hand, after which my feeling of the striking motion is essentially that it 'just happens'. I never feel as if I am

ever forcing any part of the stroke. If you look at small children, they putt naturally, they chip naturally, they swing naturally. They never think about anything else than getting the ball into the hole, and this is the most important thing. But we tour players all think there is a secret and I don't think there is a secret. The only secret is to put the ball as quickly as possible into the hole.

Ballesteros admits that some of the golfing slumps he has encountered have generally been down to the fact that he had become too technical and absorbed in his swing mechanics. Analysis has created more paralysis than perfect swings, and you may have to get yourself out of a contrived, jerky, self-conscious swing. Ballesteros is an ideal model.

Ian Woosnam is another example of 'flow' and a natural, unaffected swing. Woosnam described how he just sees the ball 'drawing into the flag' in his mind's eye, then he lets the swing take care of itself. Like Ballesteros, Woosnam's problems have arisen when he became too taken up with the mechanics rather than trusting his instinctive swing.

So, in this final stage in your modelling, take a single model like Woosnam, Ballesteros, or Fred Couples and go through the four-part modelling process, but apply it to the total swing, treating it as a single, seamless operation. When you have *become* your model - using all your senses to experience every aspect of the swing - repeat the process over and over until it becomes natural and instinctive. Vivid, multi-sensory mental rehearsal will do what endless hours of jerky, self-conscious, mechanical practice will never accomplish. This is not a matter of an easy route - you need plenty of discipline to achieve and sustain mental habits as well as physical ones - it is simply a more effective one. Learning is in small, successful steps. And success is easier than failure.

It will pay you to use this natural, effective learning process in all your golf, especially the fundamentals. In particular you will avoid the universal problem of trying to fix a swing before you have mastered the fundamentals. It harnesses natural childlike learning powers, so learning is optimal. It's quicker and longer lasting. And it means that when you do arrive at the golf course you can play and enjoy a game rather than suffer frustration and high blood pressure, with little chance of making good scores. And that is where the pleasure lies - playing, scoring, getting better, and having fun. Learning to let go can be a frightening prospect for rational adult players who have been caught in the trap of being very mechanically and position orientated. But it is worth the change. If you have to, it's well worth relearning the fundamentals from the model of your choice.

One of the difficulties many golfers have is coping with horror shots - shanks, putting 'yips', trajectories intent on hazards - which they feel do not reflect their true ability. The danger, of course, is not the fact of duff shots, which every top player is more than familiar with, but the effect these have on the rest of the play - the mental response to the shots. Greg Norman's lead of half a dozen strokes at the 1996 US Masters could have withstood a couple of horror shots and resulting bogies. But once the mental rot sets in, the self-fulfilling spiral of disaster comes into play. Rationale is no longer part of the scene, and any extraordinary thing goes.

The advantage of having a sound grasp of the fundamentals is that you have the basis on which to recover from errant shots. Coupled with this, when it comes to scoring, the lion's share in any event depends on the short game, which we cover in Chapter 6.

At one point Ben Hogan realised he had mastered the fundamentals of the swing and didn't need to worry about them. From that point he was able to abandon his earlier overthoroughness, and play more naturally. The results were dramatic. In his words: 'At about the same time I began to feel that I had the stuff to play creditable golf even when I was not at my best, my shot-making started to take on a new and more stable consistency.'

## To Sum Up . . .

This is a powerful and natural way to learn. It is well backed anecdotally in the countless caddies who have gone on to become great players, and in the way that so many top golfers developed their game as children, without the inhibitions and self-criticism that besiege the adult learner. More to the point, this seems to be the way that your super capacity, two-sided brain was intended to do the job; the way your inbuilt cybernetic goal achieving system was designed. It's the best way to learn and the best way to improve your golf. It need not be confined to the swing, or any aspect of your game. It is a powerful universal tool for personal excellence in any skill that needs to become unconscious in its operation. You can model your favourite player, for instance, mastering a bunker shot, chip or downhill putt. Having said this, the best modelling invest-ment will be in mastering a basic, sound swing. Armed then with your knowledge about goals, how to focus and main-tain your mental state and respond to pressure, you will be able to take any individual shots - which are infinite in their variety, with different lies, weather conditions, and other variable circumstances - in your stride.

With experience and practice, modelling becomes more a way of thinking, a learning attitude, than a technical process as it may initially seem. Just as children can take on different personalities more or less as the occasion demands, you will be able to use your mental free choice to draw on the best you have witnessed. Rather than relying on videos or other technology, your memory store of successful blueprints will be your modelling stock in trade. And that includes your own personal times of mastery, however rare, as well as those of the good and the great. Just as vivid mental rehearsal, allied to rapid relaxation, is a general mental skill you can use in all sorts of specific beneficial techniques, so the modelling process will prove its worth. The next chapter shows how you can build all these skills into your regular practice time.

## Masterstroke Question Clinic

***1. When I take a lesson, I seem to always play worse, even though what the pro says seems to be right. Why is this?***

When you are thinking consciously about your play you do get worse. Golf skills have to become instinctive and natural. Just like the four-part masterstroke model, the modelling exercises in this chapter are natural *learning* processes. But the principle is the same - don't analyse, copy. Don't be too self-critical, just have a go and enjoy yourself, as you did when learning as a child. Training has to become trusting.

## 2. What makes me swing so quickly?

Look at the rhythm section above, and do some remodelling based on the best players.

## 3. I have three thoughts on the backswing and two on the downswing. Is this a good idea?

Ideally, once you have mentally fixed your target you don't need to think consciously about anything. It happens as an unconscious 'motor' activity. In practice this is hard, so the next best thing is to think of just one thing. However, you are probably better thinking of a spot on the ball, your tempo, a motivating phrase or image, or your target rather than the mechanics of your swing. That's the automatic part of the operation - utilise your conscious brain to use your swing effectively to make good scores.

## 4. I know so much about the golf swing but play so badly. Why?

Golf is more about doing than knowing. Once you have made conscious decisions, about strategy, tactics, choice of club, and your target, the skill is an unconscious one. All your knowledge, at the crucial moment, is useless. In fact, by crowding your mind, it is counterproductive. Get back to basics. Knowing is part of the learning process but it has to be converted into trust. If you are a knowing type person, as we discussed in Chapter 2, get to know yourself - your beliefs, emotions, goals - rather than your swing. Follow the advice of generations of top players: look at your target, look at the ball, then swing freely.

## 5. I am really strong, with all the weight-lifting I do, yet I hit the ball nowhere. Why?

Golf is not a game of force, but of grace. Find a player,

such as Fred Couples, who relaxes and gets distance effortlessly without over-trying, and use him as your model.

**6. *Sometimes when I think of nothing and just give the ball a whack I hit a great shot. How can this be?***
See answer 4. It sounds like you have identified a great strategy. Why not do this more often? Chapter 4 described how you can recall your 'whacking' state whenever you want to.

**7. *I want to learn to play golf. Should I let my husband teach me?***
No, unless he is in the top ten in the world, and even then just use him as a model, not a teacher. Concentrate on learning rather than being taught. And, right from the start, go for excellence rather than mediocrity.

**8. *Do golf videos help?***
Yes, if you use them in a constructive way such as modelling. But you may be better with a recording of a television match, as teaching videos can be contrived - just another level of analysis.

# 6 A SPECIAL KIND OF PRACTICE

'*THE MORE* I practise,' said Gary Player, 'the luckier I get.' To improve you have got to practise. Even more important, you only establish unconscious, natural skills by repetition. But the nature and quality of your practice is more important than the quantity. And you have got to have an outcome - there must be purpose in your practice just as there is when entering a tournament. And if the game is so heavily mental how do you practise that part of it? What is quality practice - what kind of practice is needed? How do you practise mental skills?

To start with there is ordinary physical practice, of the kind you are probably very familiar with. Then there is mental practice, which involves specific techniques and routines that do not necessarily involve physical activity at all. In the first case we want to apply some of what you have already learnt about the importance of the mental game generally to your regular practice sessions, including applying the outcome principles and tests. But we also want to introduce the idea of mental practice, which, in the case of most handicap golfers, is either a foreign concept altogether or represents a disproportionately small part of their time. Then we will examine the balance between the two. If golf is 80 or 90 per cent mental, for instance, how is this reflected in your mental practice time, and do you have to change what you do physically? Practice does make perfect, provided you are practising the right things in the right way.

## Transferring Your Practice Skills

There is one problem which underlies everything you will learn about practice. Any improvement is all too often confined to practice sessions, and not transferred to competitive play and into actual scores. Even the great Ben Hogan went through frustrating years of failure during which he was more concerned with how he was hitting the ball than his score.

This is one of the pitfalls of excessive practice - a 'practice ground mentality' where the quality of the stroke matters more than scores. So although it will be useful to maximise any scarce practice time to achieve quicker and better *practice* outcomes, the big problem is how to practise in a way that affects our *higher level* outcomes of scores and handicap. Practice, if it is to be of any use, should be a means to these ends. Whoever dreams about being world number 1 at practice? If you want to be a great practiser, practise practice. If you want to be a great golfer, practise golf. The secret is to transfer your skill seamlessly from a practice to a real match situation, or even just on to a real course. As we shall see, this requires a different sort of practice.

We act as though there were two distinct mentalities: one for training, when it is acceptable to be analytical and critical, and another for playing - a trusting mentality. One is thoughtful, and the other may well be reckless and childlike, or at least automatic. This should be no surprise as each side of our brain operates in a very different way. Both mentalities have their place, of course, but all too often the training mentality is brought on to the golf course, and blocks the natural ability, flair and trust on which these sort of skills depend. Conversely we might come to a game without a sound strategy, or play shots without applying common sense, conscious thought.

Even in a training or learning mode it is sometimes necessary to abandon our critical adult mentality, and use right brain modelling methods. In the actual execution of the swing, in particular, trusting the unconscious is vital. The conscious mind simply cannot cope with all the hundreds of muscle movements and accumulated instructions in three or so seconds. Shotmaking is more an art than a science, but both sides of the game require practice. A typical practice session does not remotely simulate the real game, so as we shall see later, it is not surprising that skills are not transferred. They are the wrong skills. Mental skills travel well, so lend themselves to practice.

The pre-swing functions of the hold, addressing the ball, and routines are best practised separately from ball hitting. When these fundamentals are properly installed in your unconscious you are ready to practise hitting balls without the interference of your conscious, trying mind. Aim to have a free mind when you come to hit the golf ball. Focus on your target and scoring rather than your swing.

# Mental Practice

The average golfer will admit to spending no more than say 5 per cent of his or her time 'practising' mentally, such as doing the mental rehearsal techniques described in earlier chapters. For many the concept is completely unknown. In fact we all indulge in it to a differing extent. Imagining the worst that might happen on a particular shot, or round, for instance, or 'going over' where you went wrong, in a kind of not-very-helpful mental post mortem, is all a form of 'mental rehearsal', or practice - usually called worry or anxiety. It can affect your game, perhaps more than physical practice does. So we do engage in mental practice - remembering, imagining, rehearsing - but usually by default rather than by design. And it is usually a negative rather than positive activity. Even when you set out positively to improve your performance, as we have seen, clearly imagining something can reinforce actual behaviour *negatively* as well as positively. To start with we usually practise more misses than hits, so record plenty of the wrong kind of imagery. Ben Hogan had this to say about practice:

It really cuts me up to watch some golfers sweating away over his shots on the practice tee, throwing away his energy to no constructive purpose, nine times out of ten doing the same things he did ten years back when he first took up golf . . . If he stands out there on the practice tee 'til he's ninety, he's not going to improve. He's going to get worse and worse because he's going to get his bad habits more and more deeply ingrained.

Getting the shakes before a big tournament is probably more to do with a fertile imagination - negative mental rehearsal - than any logic or rationale. And most experienced players will admit that this can happen, however much time they have spent in physical practice. So mental practice is an easy, familiar, universal skill - we just tend to do it accidentally or unconsciously rather than as a planned, positive part of our game. You have a free will to think what you want to think. So, rather than remembering or anticipating the worst rather than the best - with the usual self-recrimination, anxiety, and horror scenarios - you can run mental practice sessions to support your outcomes. You can use existing mental skills in a different way.

## Mental baggage

Surely we can learn from past mistakes? Yes, but it is better to do this well away from a golf course, and certainly not when you should be concentrating on the shot in hand. While you might well learn from past mistakes, the chances are that unless you do this in a constructive way you will draw on the *negative emotions* of bad memories rather than pick out the helpful lessons. So we bring to each new goal unnecessary mental baggage rather than face our next challenge as if we were starting with a clean slate.

So maybe we do spend more than 5 per cent of our time on 'mental practice' after all. The point is, however, that our mental goings-on, if they happen at all, are undirected, and do not support our score and other goals. We don't control them and we certainly don't plan them into our lives. And, just like worrying when there is nothing we can do to alter a situation, it may be the worst kind of mental practice we actually need. Adrenalin and other juices are churned up but there is no real enemy on which to give vent to our feelings. So the effect of these random, undirected mental happenings is more likely to be damaging than helpful to our game, not to mention our health.

Jack Nicklaus was questioned about three shanks he hit in a tournament. 'What shanks?' was his response. Memory is selective. You can choose whether to remember good or bad shots. So get rid of some mental baggage; make your memory an asset rather than a liability.

## Using your natural mental skills

In any event, most golfers wouldn't know where to begin getting their mind into the right 'shape' to improve their game by positive mental practice. Anxiety, worry, regret, frustration, post mortems, fear, anger and other negative thought processes are part of a golfer's life, and some would say the 'pleasure' of the game! But the idea of using these natural mental 'skills' as planned, purposeful mental practice is almost unknown. You might well visualise an important game the night before, out of desperation, as an instinctive way to cope with panic or just to feel better prepared. But again, unless your visualisation is positive and empowering it can have the opposite effect to that which you had intended - if you had any intentions at all. And even if the imagined game is positive and ends in your success, the average weekly or monthly time you spend on it hardly stacks up against the importance of the mental game. So mental practice is about doing what you already naturally do (or are certainly capable of doing), but harnessing it in a purposeful, positive way to bring about specific outcomes.

## Physical v. mental?

Lots of mental practice will repay itself well. But don't look on mental and physical practice as an either/or situation. There are some situations which can only be put right with mental practice, and others which require physical practice, such as physical conditioning. And they work hand in hand. Many hours of hard physical practice can be wasted if you are compounding weaknesses based on negative beliefs, or if at the critical moment in a match you do not maintain mental control so all your physical skills are useless. David Edwards (PGA Tour) has no doubts about where to concentrate his effort:

> I got to the point where hard work didn't seem to accomplish a whole lot. I was spinning my wheels . . . So I backed off on working hard and focused more on the mental part.

## Evaluating practice time and effort

To get the best balance you will need to evaluate your practice. If time and effort are the inputs and hard scores or a lower handicap the outputs, how effective is orthodox physical practice? Does it have a material, measurable effect, not just in practice mode but on your game, and especially under pressure when it usually counts most? Looked at another way, how many times has trying harder, or changing your technique, simply not brought about any positive change? Have you found, for instance, that there are *diminishing returns* - that is, you don't get the improvement you hope for out of each extra increment of time and effort? Sadly, that is in the very nature of even the most conscientious practice. On its own, *at any degree,* physical, technical practice will not solve your big problems. Use the chart on page 190 (Figure 6a) to measure your practice *inputs.* Amend it to suit your specific *output* needs. The same sort of chart, you will see, (figure 6b), can also be used to measure your performance on the golf course. Don't forget to congratulate yourself, and perhaps give yourself a reward when you play well. Evaluation can be a positive part of your learning. And learn to trap your successes in your mind - savour them, they belong to you, and are assets that can be used again and again. That way you will get the most value out of your practice.

## Flow and 'hot streaks'

Think back now to specific occasions when your *mental state* accounted for big differences in performance - however unexpected or isolated such occasions have been. You may have actually surprised yourself on a particularly difficult shot, or exceeded all expectations in your final score, with the same body, brain and clubs as usual. Many golfers are familiar with long 'hot streaks' - runs of effortless, superb play - in a state of 'flow'. Were these priceless times connected with endless hours of effort or were they linked with a relaxed, fearless or confident state of mind? Inducing and controlling these mental states does not come by doing more and trying harder. It is only possible through mental processes, as you saw in Chapter 4. And because the mind is prone to good and bad *habits* just like the body, it requires practice - mental rather than physical practice.

Each kind of practice is important and interdependent, just as in the mind-body partnership we have already discussed. In most cases the mental side is seriously neglected and improvements well within our potential are unknowingly forfeited. So when it comes to balancing practice time the very fact of the disproportionate effect of the mind on all our performance tells us where to direct our attention. We need to develop mental *skills*, and that requires mental practice.

# Creating The Perfect Round

You can use mental practice to create a perfect round. Here is what to do, and the benefits you will enjoy. Use the 3-2-1 method (see Chapter 4) to relax and get into the best 'alpha' state of mind for mental practice. The more familiar you become with this process, the more you will look forward to it and the more effective will be the mental techniques you use. In this state (level 1) you might wish, for example, to play a whole round - perhaps in full competitive conditions, maybe in foul weather conditions.

This form of mental practice, applied to a whole game, a job interview, or perhaps a speech you have to make, is particularly useful in creating confidence and removing unnatural levels of stress before any important, perhaps unfamiliar occasion. In this case a realistic visualisation (one that tricks the brain into believing you are playing an actual round of competitive golf, for instance) needs to cover not just the shots, but the events before you start, the moments before the first tee shot, the long walks between shots, and the after-game accolades. It can also include problems and set-backs to add realism - provided you always finish with the final outcome you want.

Chris Evert, the Wimbledon champion tennis player, would visualise a match rather than just (as many tennis players do) individual strokes, including her opponent and the tactics she would adopt. Similarly, Duncan Goodhue, the Olympic swimming gold medallist, would lie down and visualise - with sounds and feelings - the whole successful swim before embarking immediately on putting his sensory blueprint into practice. If you have ever fantasised about winning in some great event, while driving your car or lying in bed, you will have used the same mental skills. Now you can start to practise and hone these mental skills, so that your imagery becomes more real and powerful. So rather than just engage in Walter Mitty type dreaming, you can now direct your mental practice towards specific goals. Remember also what you learnt in Chapter 4 about switching submodalities to fine-tune your performance and state of mind. You can always get better, and it starts in your imagination.

## *Tricks with time from your armchair*

You will find that you can condense the whole process into a fraction of the time it would take to play an actual game, or for that matter the sort of time you might well spend in actual practice. So mental practice has special timing implications. You can run through an important shot many times, for instance, in a 20 minute period. When people talk of seeing their whole lives pass before them in near death experiences we get some idea of this amazing facility of the mind to fast forward or backward. And there are even more practical time benefits of mental practice. You don't have to spend all the time travelling to and from the practice ground, putting up with the weather, and the rest of the inconvenience that ordinary practice entails. Time is a big problem with many serious golfers, and their families. A smarter mental approach to the game, both as regards practice time and also in balancing the sport with other people and priorities in your life, goes a long way towards overcoming the problem. Armchair mental practice is an effective time management tool.

## Perfect shots

Rather than visualising a whole match or round, you might want to concentrate a practice session on a specific aspect of your game, or even a specific hole or bunker shot on your home course. By either recalling actual memories of the perfect shot, or creating them (remember the process of modelling a perfect swing), you will have a blueprint upon which to base your practice session. Experience each sense, or modality - seeing , hearing and feeling - first in turn then together. As is the case in real life, the behaviour will become etched on your mental hard disk. The more 're-cordings' you make, the stronger will be the 'muscle memory', and the more natural and instinctive will be the skills when you get on to the course. Consistent shots produce consistent rounds, so any specific mental practice of this sort will be congruent with your score outcomes.

## Practising success

Remember that in all your mental practice you are not (unless you want to be particularly mischievous) rehearsing failure, but success. So whatever your actual track record to date of horror shots or rounds, with regular mental practice the positive recordings will soon outbalance the negative ones. Being more recent, in any event, just like actual recent memories, they will tend to have greater impact. You cannot erase hard disk horror memories, but you can *counterbalance* a lot of negative mental baggage in a purposeful hour or so of mental practice.

It remains for you to ensure that these practice sessions are so real that your brain cannot tell the difference between them and actual super performance in real life. This is why both relaxation and a general skill in using the techniques - which, like any skill, physical or mental, comes with time and practice - is important. It may also help to do practice separately on each modality - seeing, hearing and feeling - so that you become more sensitive to each, and particularly in using the sense or senses that you do not naturally prefer. Spend some time, for instance, on all the sounds associated with a pleasant success memory, if normally your main recall is visual. Or concentrate on the feelings, if you would not normally do so. You can then go further in exploring the submodalities, or qualities of these representations. For example look at the colour, clarity and focus of the sights, and hear the volume, speed and pitch of the sounds.

All this is what makes up your experience, and what creates the impact of a memory or anticipated event, and your state of mind. If you like, this is your personal raw material data store for creating what you want to create in your mind. Then, as we have seen, subjective thought tends to become objective reality. Having explored memories by individual modality, then submodality, it is important then to bring them all together, thus creating the brain 'reality' - real life is always multi-sensory - you are after. This powerful mental skill can be applied to all your practice.

## What To Practise

When describing *how* to practise we have used several examples of *what* to practise. Here we will summarise and comment on the main applications for mental practice:

○ 'internalising' your outcomes;

○ preparing for a big game;

○ problem shots;

○ changing negative beliefs;

○ holes with negative memories;

○ becoming familiar with a course;

○ experiencing competitive play, or a specific partner who makes you nervous;

○ 'experiencing' difficult weather conditions;

○ preparing your state of mind;

○ playing with clubs you avoid using; and

○ testing out scenarios such as winning, turning professional etc.

## Internalising outcomes

You can use visualisation to imprint clear, vivid outcomes on your mind. You have already learnt the tests of a well-formed outcome, and these for the most part can be treated as common-sense, conscious ways to increase your chances of achieving any goal. Mental rehearsal supplements and internalises these, but decide on your outcomes and do the tests first. By deciding in each case on the sensory evidence (what you will see, hear and feel) of your outcome achievement, you can incorporate it as part of your visualisation in mental practice sessions.

Be creative. When savouring success enjoy all the indirect pleasure of your achievement, such as the praise and respect of others, and your new-found confidence and self-esteem. If, for example, your ambition was to play off scratch, you will need to experience every aspect of the new 'you'. You need to experience what you now *are* as well as what you have *done*. What sort of things would you do and say, what would people say to you, how would other parts of your life be affected, how would you approach your game as a scratch player? If you can't *imagine* it, it is doubtful you will pull it off.

By experiencing all this inwardly, if need be drawing on models other than yourself in a role-playing way, the outcome will become firmly etched in your mind - your brain will *believe* it. This will paint a more realistic brain picture - real events can never be isolated from other parts of our life. At the same time the perceived pleasure will act as a strong subconscious motivator towards the target goal.

## Preparing for the big game

As well as mentally 'registering' your target, mental rehearsal will help prepare your state of mind, taking the heat out of an anxious situation, and giving you confidence. The effect is just as though you were so familiar with such a situation that you simply take it in your stride. This familiarity comes from the brain not distinguishing between actual happenings and the events you have rehearsed vividly in your mind. In some cases this has resulted in top players having a sense of *déjà vu* when winning a major event.

Gary Player spoke of *knowing* he would win when flying into a tournament and seeing his name on the scoreboard. For him, it was as though it had already happened, which, of course, to his brain it had. Other players have spoken of a certainty of success, even during the game when actual scores and setbacks told a very different story.

What is sometimes put down to premonition, super confidence, or single-mindedness is more likely to be a skilled use of mental rehearsal which gives the player the right attitude and self-belief. We described in Chapter 3 the technique for bringing about a belief change, which you recall involved mental rehearsal, and the same technique was used to anchor a mental state in Chapter 4. Use these in your practice, perhaps concentrating on one belief and one 'state' each week.

Preparing for any event you are concerned about is an important function of visualisation, as there are certain situations that you cannot realistically practise. The pressure of an important tournament, for instance, cannot be properly simulated on a practice ground, or in a more friendly competitive situation. This is why a special occasion can be such a disaster; we are mentally completely unprepared, however many hours of practice we have put in. Mental practice solves all this, and you can prepare for any level or type of pressure - literally *anything you can imagine* - whether it is a particular hazard or difficult hole, your opening tee shot, or the closing strokes of a tournament. You will take the big games in your stride.

## Correcting weaknesses

You can use visualisation for specific shots you want to improve. Use what you have learnt so far. First, if you can recall making the shot once, you have a personal mental resource upon which to draw - your own blueprint of excellence. Most experienced golfers can recall a whole variety of super shots - they just don't make enough at the time they are needed. Alternatively, go back to Chapter 5 and see how modelling others can help. Either way, the imagination is a powerful, flexible tool.

Having perfected the shot you want internally, practice is just that - repeating the successful shot until it becomes well registered subconsciously. As well as creating the muscle memories, or mental strategy, you will draw upon as you 'let go' in the real game, this will also give you confidence. On the course, provided you don't try to rationalise what you are doing, but rather trust your inbuilt system, you can expect remarkable improvement.

Using this technique you can therefore set up mental practice sessions for different shots, concentrating on those that are weak, or that you have a low self-image about. Leave your good shots alone until you have achieved overall mental control of your game.

## Changing disempowering beliefs

In Chapter 3 you learnt a belief change process that involved recalling three successful memories to support a 'preferred' belief that would help you rather than hinder you in achieving your goals. Use mental practice to establish those behaviours, and strengthen your new belief. A long-held 'I am a slicer' type belief might need lots of 'proof' to convince your subconscious mind that you are now different. The only proof, of course, is actual electro-chemical changes you make in your brain by clearly visualising the supporting behaviour. That is the only currency of the brain. It likes to have sensory evidence of a belief that leaves no room for other 'interpretations'.

In summary, you can practise anything mentally that you might physically, and a lot more, such as pressure situations that only arise infrequently. The big difference is speed and convenience, and the fact that you spare your brain negative failure experiences. In short, mental practice is much more effective and enjoyable.

# Applying Your Mind To Physical Practice

So, how can you apply all this to conventional, physical practice? Mental practice is a world apart from the orthodox practice sessions we are so familiar with. The rules are very different. It seems that in some circumstances extended physical practice can actually be detrimental to your game. On the one hand bad habits are reinforced every time you practise them - just like crossing over your hands when driving. And the bad behaviour creates the negative beliefs which simply reinforce the vicious performance spiral. Worse than that, when improvements do occur in practice they may not be transferred to the course, especially in pressure situations. So new frustrations and self-image knocks occur.

Having said this, a lot can be done to gain maximum benefit from physical practice. Having already learnt the principles and techniques of the mental game, it is a matter of applying common sense and a bit of right brain creativity. Here are some of the things you can apply from what you have already learnt.

## Goal-setting

Practice, like any other activity, should have a purpose. This is what the great Jack Nicklaus said: 'All my life I've tried to hit practice shots with great care. I try to have a clear-cut purpose in mind on every swing. I always practice as I intend to play.'

All too often practice time is spent in almost random ball bashing without specific practice outcomes. Bear in mind the hierarchy of goals model in Chapter 2, in which the test of any outcome, at any level, is whether it contributes to your higher level goals. Few golfers will be satisfied with practice performance that does not translate into actual scores, a lower handicap and probably competitive success at some level or other.

Having said that, specific stepping-stone practice outcomes will help you get more out of the time and effort you put in. Rather than randomly hitting buckets full of balls why not limit yourself to perhaps a couple of dozen balls, but follow a learning plan, carefully recording your performance over a period? Decide what you want to get out of every session. Make your outcome positive, specific, etc., as you did for your overall outcomes. In particular, don't be distracted by well-meaning partners or those who offer free advice.

## Routine

Keep to an agreed pre-swing or pre-putt routine as we discussed in Chapter 4, so that this becomes instinctive when playing for real, and your practice is more transferable to the game. This is one kind of physical practice that does not need to involve misses, and a regular routine is vital for consistency. Doug Sanders, whose famous 18 inch missed putt at the British Open more than a quarter of a century ago was probably the most memorable in golfing history, spoke recently with passion on the subject. Asked whether he was still affected by it he answered that sometimes he can go a full five minutes without thinking about it! But another comment was particularly significant: 'I did so many things different to my normal routine.' This is very much part of the mental game, and is repaid by both physical and mental practice.

## Simulating real play

The difference between practice and real play is extraordinary. For example while in practice you use the same club over and over again, in play you do just the opposite. While in practice you repeat the same stroke, real play is all about variety and uncertainty. The familiar hazards on the course are nowhere to be seen on the practice range. While you religiously execute a pre-shot routine in play, you readily dispense with it in practice, as balls hurtle off into the distance. While you repeatedly analyse and correct your swing in practice this can be a disastrous habit in a match. Not surprisingly your practice is the worst kind of simulation, and the course might be a moon landscape in comparison.

The more your practice simulates real play the less you will face the universal problem this chapter started with of transferring what you can easily do in practice to a competitive game. Why not do in practice what you know you will be doing on the course? For example:

○ *Trust* your swing.

○ Develop unconscious skills rather than honing your critical powers.

○ Make every shot count, as it does in play.

○ Focus on the shot in hand.

○ Keep to a routine.

○ Vary your shots.

○ Vary your clubs.

○ Change your distances.

○ Have shot targets, and practise maintaining the image as you play your stroke.

○ Set up something competitive, or at least compete with yourself.

○ Design scores and results into your practice.

○ Have session outcomes each time you practice.

Ben Hogan knew a few things about meaningful practice. He once discovered a slight waywardness in his fairway wood shots when he was tired, so he deliberately tired himself on the practice ground so that he could study the phenomenon and correct it. Use your ingenuity to get as near as you can to playing mode. Use your mind.

## Tackling weaknesses

Tackle specific weaknesses one at a time. Be ready to give over a full practice session to one specific weakness, so your mind does not become crowded and you learn in small chunks. And confine your conscious thinking about the problem to between shots rather than when making the shots. Practise emptying your mind when actually playing the stroke. The very skill of switching from a conscious mode to trusting and letting go when executing the shot is an invaluable skill for the real game. Unless you can empty your mind of anything other than your target when making the swing, or at least confining your thoughts to one positive or neutral thing (such as a spot on the ball, a word or feeling, or an image of the target) your swing will break down under any sort of pressure. Your practice can also include visualising your target internally and retaining the image. Add a mental dimension to all your physical practice. Then you can measure your hits and misses over a period and thus monitor your improvement *in practice conditions*. Don't kid yourself that you are practising *golf* - golf is only played on a golf course, and there is always a score. It's a game, not a series of physical exercises. Just make sure that your practice outcomes support your golf outcomes, as in your hierarchy of goals.

## On the practice green

On the practice green you can similarly set specific goals. You may decide to concentrate on chips and set a target to sink two - or one or three - in a session. Again, once your target is clear in its hierarchy - first the shot, then your session performance, then your improvement over a period - you will have a purpose to your practice that links with your higher golf outcomes, such as to be a better chipper and, higher up, to lower your handicap or win the monthly medal. Measuring over a period takes some of the randomness out of the activity, and a documented improvement, however small, will do a lot for your self-esteem in that area of the game. By measuring chips sunk, you get into the habit of going for what you actually want rather than having a general target area. That is, you stick to the sound principle of going for the smallest possible target. And these are the types of shots that make birdies.

Every ball you sink, of course, becomes a candidate for mental rehearsal - a model upon which you can draw for further use. So you will soon build up plenty of raw material for mental practice, and the two modes of practice will become mutually supportive. As we have seen, your repeated mental imagery of the successes will help to counterbalance the hundreds of misses your self-image has to cope with.

## *Targeting the fringe for pace practice*

Use what you have learnt about the mental game in planning your practice goals. In distance practice for long putts, for example, you might choose to putt towards the edge of the green rather than the hole. By putting to the fringe from all possible distances you will get to look at the fringe and react to it instinctively with each stroke. The idea is to get to the edge of the green without going into the fringe, and develop a feel for pace, which is the key to long putts. You can still set up some directional target but the important difference is that the brain does not record obvious repeated 'misses' which are a feature of long putt practice to the hole. Although consciously you may not be concerned about missing nine out of every ten putts, claiming that you are just practising 'technique', your unconscious mind is not so easily kidded. It will register misses in great volume and file them away somewhere. The important thing is to have an interim goal (leading towards your score and handicap goals) - in this case to judge distance on long putts - that is specific and  measurable.

The special significance of short putt practice is that you record repeated actual success memories - quite rare in physical practice - that are important for your confidence. Any 'success' practice is important to boost self-belief, of course, and in the case of very short putts there is less of an advantage in mental practice.

Practise mental target visualisation also in normal practice times; that is, getting a clear internal image of where you want the ball to go. Remember to explore all the modalities, not just visual. Hearing the sound of the ball hitting the back of the cup, and the precise feelings you link with a super putt or short shot will all help to reinforce the internal target. There is a mental dimension to everything you do, and there should be no boundary between mental and physical practice. You are practising mind-body skills.

## Putting: to practise or not to practise?

Some notable top golfers spend little time in putting practice. Bobby Locke and Ben Crawshaw were not ones for practising putting, and Sam Snead spent little time on any aspect of practice. Peter Thomson remarks that of his generation, Ben Hogan, insofar as practice is concerned, was the exception rather than the rule. The point is that good putting is primarily a matter of attitude and routine. For a seasoned player the routine is as ingrained in the unconscious as walking or climbing stairs, which is not something we tend to practise. And attitude is not something that comes with physical practice, in any case, however conscientious you are, but is to do with how you think.

There is not even an accepted standard putting technique that your hours of practice can aspire to. You will find there are as many styles as the personalities that take up the putters. The first rule is, of course, 'If it ain't broke, don't fix it.' In the case of your putting, if it *is* broke the chances are that the problem is mental rather than mechanical in any case. If mechanics is the problem you are back to fundamentals as with the swing, and you can just as well do your modelling practice without a ball at home. If it's attitude and feel you want to develop, mental practice techniques fit the bill far better. Top players who don't physically practise putting usually have a strong mental game, and might well practise mentally more than others.

## State control

Getting and keeping in the right state of mind is not nearly as difficult on the practice range as in a match. But physical practice still has its mental side. It's just that different emotions and beliefs may be at work: 'I'm brilliant when practising on my own;' 'I'm useless in tournament play.' This is where you can benefit from practising state control first in a non-pressure setting. By the time you get on to the course you should be able to induce a chosen resource - such as calmness, confidence, patience, courage, etc. - by applying a simple anchor as in Chapter 4. You fix these anchors during your mental practice sessions, so your live practice time, during which you try out one resource at a time, is complementary to what you do back at home or in your lunch break at work. Combine your mental resource practice with pre-swing routines. Unless you have control in practice mode, first mentally (ready relaxation and clear multi-sensory images), then in non-pressure physical practice (concentration, target focus, mental attitude, letting go, etc.), you are unlikely to have control when you most need it. And controlling how you feel requires a lot of practice for most people.

Quality practice, both physical and mental, and a confident state of mind are closely linked, and one feeds on the other. The harder you prepare for anything, the higher your level of confidence about it and the more you will be ready for pressure. So you will perform better. Goal-orientation and a strong self-belief, as well as practice, will also form part of your preparation. As we have seen, these are within your control.

## Pre-round preparation

What about warming up immediately before a game? In this case you are mainly concerned with getting into the right mental state. It's too late to start solving big problems. You have got to let go and enjoy yourself. After doing some long putts - perhaps going for the fringes from different distances as above - finish with a few nice short putts, applying to each your full putting routine. Savour the feelings of success. If on your long shots you are doing well, just believe you will do the same on your round, and do not tempt fortune with extended practice. Think about your *outcome* for your practice - low scores, pleasure, perhaps some fun, but not self-flagellation. If things are not so good, just believe that you are saving your best for the game. Mentally, you can actually have it both ways. Make your pre-round practice an enjoyable win-win warm-up time. You can think what you like, and the real purpose is to get physically prepared and into a relaxed, empowering, score-making state of mind.

## How To Use Your Time

We have established the importance of mental practice and how you can use it in your game, and suggested ways in which your normal practice can also benefit. So, how do you spread your time in terms of different types of shot, and your long game as opposed to your short game? In terms of instruction to handicapped golfers the present split is something like the following:

| **Physical** (90 per cent) | **Mental** (10 per cent) |
|---|---|
| Full swing (about 80 per cent) | 'Think positive' (about 9 per cent) |
| Short game (about 10 per cent) | Other (about 1 per cent) |

    Putting

    Chip

    Pitch

    Sand

    Speciality

This reflects the obsession with the technicalities of the swing we have already talked about, some ignorance about which types of shot produce scores, as well as ignorance generally of the mental aspects of the game. The same groups of golfers who reflect this actual practice time (and in many cases the instructors who teach them) will readily agree that golf is 80 or 90 per cent mental. So something has got turned upside down.

Even ignoring the importance of mental factors, the statistics on actual scoring speak for themselves. Almost all golfers make their scores in a round by hitting about one-third full shots, and about two-thirds less than full shots - just the reverse of the typical effort and time put into practice. You will find similar statistics based on which clubs are used. Again, the driver through to the wedge, used in a full swing, accounts for little more than one-third of club use.

The message is the same right at the top, whatever attention the television commentators give to those long, macho tee shots. The average top US tour player hits only 12 greens per round (i.e. misses one out of three greens). The same sample group hits only 9.6 fairways per round. So why are these people at the top, making low final scores and earning lots of money? The answer is that they have outstanding games on and around the greens - where it matters. After all, a 5-foot putt counts the same as a 270-yd drive. And the woods are full of balls from long drivers. You can measure how you actually use your time in off-course practice using the chart in Figure 6a. Figure 6b can be used to measure your on-course progress.

## Embarrassing questions

This raises some embarrassing questions for teachers as well as serious golfers. Either golfers practise the full swing most of the time because they don't want low scores (which come from the short game); or they are gullible to the golf instruction industry which thrives on perpetual analysis of the swing. Or they just follow the crowds, without thinking about the common sense of what they are doing or not doing. Or maybe the big shots have more macho appeal. In any case, if scores and a lower handicap are the objectives, the practice regime of the average club golfer is not too clever. For years Jack Nicklaus never figured in the top statistics of fairways hit, greens reached, longest drives and the like. But he was number 1 in tournament and money wins, and - significantly - in fewest putts.

The mental game, as well as embracing unconscious motor skills, also includes being bright rather than dumb. The choice is yours. You can practise beating a ball as far

## Figure 6a: Practice Record

| | Time Spent | | | | | | |
|---|---|---|---|---|---|---|---|
| Putting Stroke Practice | | | | | | | |
| Putting Distance Practice | | | | | | | |
| Chipping | | | | | | | |
| Pitching/Short | | | | | | | |
| Pitching/Long | | | | | | | |
| Bunkers | | | | | | | |
| Full Swing/Woods | | | | | | | |
| Full Swing/Irons | | | | | | | |
| Speciality Shots | | | | | | | |
| Mechanics | | | | | | | |
| Mental Practice | | | | | | | |
| Physical Conditioning | | | | | | | |
| | | | | | | | |
| Totals | | | | | | | |

## Figure 6b: Round By Round Scores

| | | | | | | |
|---|---|---|---|---|---|---|
| Date | | | | | | |
| Putts | | | | | | |
| Up and Down in Two | | | | | | |
| Sand Save | | | | | | |
| Greens in Regulation | | | | | | |
| Fairways Hit in Regulation | | | | | | |
| Score | | | | | | |

as you can. Or you can practise getting consistent low scores. And for that you have to start using your brain on the right side as well as the left.

## Horses for golf courses

Once you start to think about these simple facts, and you can use your own experience if you doubt the international research, you can make your own decisions about the time and effort you want to put into different parts of your game. You don't need my help. Based on the above, it would make sense to spend two-thirds of your practice time on the all-important short game. In terms of individual short shots, this will depend a lot on your individual needs and practice objectives. A particular shot, for instance, might cause you more pressure than others, and might be the subject of a disempowering belief about your ability in that specific stroke or hazard situation. So it's horses for courses. Although you will only solve this mentally, there may be a period during which it gets more physical time as well. That is where clear outcomes are important, at every level, including specific practice goals. Otherwise, as a general rule, maintain your strength and work on your weaknesses. Keep in mind your higher golf goals - scores, handicap, fun - rather than making practice an end in itself. Your own goals and specific needs, rather than suggestions you read in magazines, will be the best basis for allocating your practice time.

## Outputs for inputs

There is another important question when deciding on how you spend your practice time. Having divided your time between physical and mental practice, then approximately between your short and long game, it is important to establish how amenable certain types of shot are to practice. In other words, what outputs will you get in return for your inputs of time and energy? As a simple example, what are the respective benefits of practising 3-ft as against 6-ft - or, for that matter, 12-ft putts? Specifically, what *improvement* (in your hit rate) would an hour, or ten hours, at each produce? If you are serious about your practice planning and recording, you will produce exactly this sort of information. Use Figure 6c as a guide.

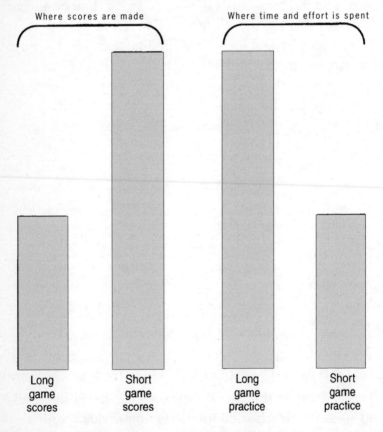

**Figure 6c** Output for Inputs

There is a vast difference between practising 3-ft putts as against 12-ft putts. In the former case the large majority of your practice will be a success - hits. In the latter case most of your practice will be of failure - misses. As we have seen, these experiences are recorded on the hard disk of your brain. In the one case you are becoming more skilled at and familiar with succeeding, whereas in the other case you are becoming more and more experienced at missing targets.

One way to counteract this is to mentally rehearse plenty of hits so that they become dominant in your brain. In a real game, where misses are a fact of life, this is the ideal way to overcome this mental phenomenon and maintain your positive beliefs for every new shot. But in practice, when you don't have to so obviously miss, you are better rethinking your objectives and strategy for improvement.

If, in the case of long putts, the objective is to instinctively get your direction and length right, can you achieve these interim objectives without so obviously missing holes? As we saw earlier you don't need a hole to practise direction and pace. You can use the fringe of the green, a tee or a sweet paper. So, however misses are 'registered', they will not be associated with a real hole in a real game - that is, with misses or failure. Your subconscious mind therefore does not have to deal with possibly hundreds or thousands of the wrong mind-signals when all it wants is to do what you have done before and can do again.

The same principle can be applied to other short shots. If an interim sand shot objective is to get well clear of the sand cleanly and consistently (and that is a good score producing interim practice goal), why introduce a hole and just about guarantee 100 per cent failure when that is the last thing you need to cope with? If distance is the practice objective, then decide on a target that will measure distance, without the associations of a tiny hole in the ground. Base your practice inputs on the learning outputs you want.

## Practising smarter, not harder

Be selective and ingenious in your practice. Sadly, brute effort is not repaid, nor is will power and discipline. If you are doing the wrong things it doesn't matter how sincere or dedicated you are. This is what Jack Nicklaus said:

> Sheer quantity of practice alone will not make a golfer a good putter. Without feel, touch and timing it wouldn't have mattered how many hundreds of putts I'd hit on the practice putting green. Consequently, I've never practised beyond that point where I knew I was doing what I wanted to do with my stroke. This goal has always been the product of a consistent rhythm or tempo, marked by the putter face making solid and square contact with the ball. The physical feel and the mind picture this produces is one of great fluidity between my hands and the putterhead. Once I attain these goals in a practice session, I quit, even if I have stroked only a handful of putts. By continuing beyond that point, I risk becoming too mechanical or losing my sense of touch. You too should be aware of spoiling a good thing by overdoing it.

Nicklaus's comments closely reflect the school of thought we met earlier that says you should not overpractise putting mechanics. Everything about the unconscious automatic system we have learnt so far adds sense to this idea. You don't practise breathing, walking or tying your shoelaces. Once you have internalised the mechanics of such skills, you just *do* them. If you think about them you tend to get worse rather than better. If you seriously practised climbing up and down stairs for any length of time, thinking about what your legs were doing, for example, you might well break your neck. Speaking about Ben Crenshaw, Harvey Penick said: 'When he was a boy I wouldn't let him practise too much for fear he might find out how to do something wrong.' Now you have got the information, you can make your own decision about how to spend your practice. But always find time to develop childlike, intuitive skills.

## Practising basic skills

To get this right you need *general* practice in using your basic sensory skills internally, and being able to relax and 'turn off' for the purpose. This is what produces the necessary clarity and realism of the imagery. This is learning how to learn the way your mind does it best. Then your specific practice will cover the shots, or any other behaviour that supports your preferred belief. So it pays to get into the habit of spending regular time exercising your subjective mind in the ways I have described. Using the 3-2-1 method, specific belief changes, for instance, can be made through repeatedly practising the actual new behaviour, as described in Chapter 3. For example, you can practise playing off a lower handicap and so align your beliefs to the new low handicap 'you'. Then, when pursuing your six-month or whatever goal, instead of being hampered by negative beliefs, your actual performance will be supported, in a self-fulfilling way, by empowering beliefs. Go back to the beliefs you identified that needed to be changed, and the behaviours that would support your new beliefs. Similarly, decide on the empowering states of mind you need to improve your game, and establish reliable anchors as you learnt in Chapter 4. You will then know how best to use your basic mental skills in practice sessions, or in any spare moment at home, at work or when travelling.

# Masterstroke Question Clinic

### 1. Why do I play better in practice than I do playing on the course?

There is hardly any comparison, and I have shown that conventional practice does not properly simulate the real game. Use the techniques I have suggested to minimise this difference, and in any event regular mental practice routines will overcome this fundamental problem. Try and *create* pressure, giving yourself difficult practice targets that stretch you, or introducing competition with friends.

### 2. If I practise so much, why does my game not improve?

For the same reasons, combined with the fact that we usually practice failure rather than success. Balance your practice between mental and physical, and also to reflect the way scores are made.

### 3. I would like to practise more but I get bored when I do. What can I do about it?

Follow the advice in this chapter, and get to know the pleasure and effectiveness of mental practice. Also set goals and some form of self-competition to bring more meaning and enjoyment to your normal practice sessions.

### 4. I'm trying so hard yet getting nowhere. What can I do?

Stop trying, and follow the above suggestions about practice. You don't *try* to pour a cup of coffee, or put the cat out at night. Golf skills call on the same automatic mind-body skills which, once learnt, you don't need to consciously think about. There may well be other problems which you will identify from the previous chapters, so that even your trying may be concentrated on the wrong things.

### 5. I know that practice makes perfect but I don't have the time. What can I do?

You can practise mentally far more *time efficiently*, without disrupting your lifestyle, and you can follow the suggestions for getting more out of any physical practice you can fit into your busy life. You will not attain perfection, but practice makes *permanent* - it helps establish long-standing habits. Go for quality rather than quantity, and direct your practice towards specific learning goals.

### 6. Joe never ever practises yet plays so well. How come?

You are probably referring to physical practice. It sounds as though Joe is doing a few things right in his mental game - like trusting his swing and getting the best out of his present abilities.

### 7. How much time should I spend practising?

If you practise the right things in the right way, which is what this chapter is all about, you can spend as much or as little time as you like and get benefit. The main thing is to practise to play - for score or handicap results - and not for the sake of it. Watch out, however, for any adverse effect on other areas of your life - check back in Chapter 2 to ecology of outcomes and the hierarchy of goals.

### 8. *I love to hit the ball a long way and I practise with my driver all the time. Is this good?*

It's fine if you do it for the pleasure but, as we have explained, it will not do much for your scores. It's as far away from the real scoring, where you change clubs all the time and depend so much on the short game as could be imagined.

# AFTERWORD: THE BIG GAME

What you have learnt about the mental side of golf has far wider application in other areas of your life. All the principles you have met, and most of the techniques, could be applied to other sports, and hobbies, as well as to work situations and family life. Some sports, for example, have used visualisation techniques for a number of years to the extent that they are now a fairly standard part of coaching. Golf has lagged behind in this respect, although this is changing fast. Similarly, some of the goal achievement ideas we have covered have been practised in business for many years, although the idea of mental rehearsal is still suspect for most managers and business people, educated and trained as they are in a left-brain dominant way.

It works both ways: there are lessons we can bring to our golf from other parts of life, and there are in turn lessons we can draw from golf and apply elsewhere. Golf is a sort of microcosm of life, in which the whole range of emotions is experienced. There are dreams, hopes, setbacks, joy and anger, fears and challenges, despair and elation. It is like a school or a college at which we gain knowledge and qualifications to venture into the real world. Golf teaches us a lot about the human character. Play a round of golf with someone and you will get to know them more intimately than you might from years of dinner parties. Because it is so exacting and unforgiving, it comes closer to the game of life than most other games or sports.

As well as preparing for the big golf game you can use mental rehearsal techniques to prepare for:

○ an interview;

○ an examination;

○ an important business meeting;

○ a sales appointment;

○ a social situation you are uneasy about;

○ a speech or public presentation; and

○ any 'first time' occasion you are worried about.

It takes little imagination to think of similar situations where this sort of mental control could pay big dividends. The same sinking feeling can grip you as you are approaching the boss's door, or getting up to give a speech, or preparing to discipline a member of your staff, as when you face that first tee, or last critical putt. The same chemicals are at work in your brain and body, and the same familiar feelings in your stomach or wherever they do their work. In such moments all your professionalism and skill can evaporate and you can become a dithering incompetent. But you don't have to feel unhappy, or depressed, or helpless, unless you want to be. Controlling your state of mind, how you feel, is a mental skill you can learn and apply to your golf in the relative safety of a golf course, then start reaping its benefits in every other part of your life.

Use NLP techniques to prepare for any ordeal you have to face. In many cases this will be a godsend as you have no choice but to hold the meeting, make the speech, or whatever you have to go through with. But it is far more positive than that. You may well find yourself accepting opportunities you would previously have turned down, sometimes ingeniously, in a self-fulfilling conformity to your self-beliefs ('I am no good speaking in front of a crowd/group,' 'I'm no good handling conflict,' etc.). By breaking out of negative self-belief patter, you will embark on an upward spiral of self-development and personal performance. You may even look out for opportunities in the areas you were previously terrified about, and all sorts of new possibilities will emerge.

Whatever its frustrations, golf has probably kept more people sane than psychiatrists have. It is therapeutic, educational, and mentally stimulating. It's a lesson in living. You can apply what you have learnt in the school of golf mastery to radically change any part of your life. The techniques you have learnt will help you to:

○ make decisions;

○ control how you feel;

○ believe in yourself;

○ understand people better;

○ overcome problems;

○ forget failures and set-backs;

○ focus on the important things;

○ handle pressure;

○ live in body-mind harmony;

○ stretch and motivate yourself for new challenges; and

○ turn dreams into reality.

In the Life Content model we identified different categories of outcome which largely reflect our different personalities and preferences. Things we want:

○ to know;

○ to do;

○ to have or get;

○ to be; and

○ that affect relationships.

Whatever categories your personal goals fit into, if you carried out the exercise in Chapter 2 you will no doubt already have identified a number of goals other than golf. These are the shots and holes of an even bigger game, and the winnings, if you get it right, can be far more significant than on the most lucrative professional circuits. As Gary Player used to say, a dropped stroke can never be redeemed. Like time itself, it is lost forever. And this philosophy helps to explain his remarkable tenacity, discipline and self-control.

In another rather sobering metaphorical way, we just get to play *one round*. So we've got to get it right, whether in the score of worthwhile achievement or the pleasure of a full, enjoyable game - in quality of life. The scenery. The company. The challenge. The flow. The learning. The growth. The purpose of it all. And if we need to have some practice for this single round of life, or the odd dress rehearsal, the game of golf - at least the mental game - fits the requirement as well as anything else.

# INDEX

# Piatkus Business Books

Piatkus Business Books have been created for people who need expert knowledge readily available in a clear and easy-to-follow format. All the books are written by specialists in their field. They will help you improve your skills quickly and effortlessly in the workplace and on a personal level.

Titles include:

*General Management and Business Skills*

**Be Your Own PR Expert: the complete guide to publicity and public relations**   Bill Penn
**Complete Conference Organiser's Handbook, The**   Robin O'Connor
**Complete Time Management System, The**   Christian H. Godefroy and John Clark
**Confident Decision Making**   J. Edward Russo and Paul J H Schoemaker
**Continuous Quality Improvement**   Alasdair White
**Corporate Culture**   Charles Hampden-Turner
**Energy Factor, The: how to motivate your workforce**   Art McNeil
**Firing On All Cylinders: the quality management system for high-powered corporate performance**   Jim Clemmer with Barry Sheehy
**How to Implement Change in Your Company**   John Spencer and Adrian Pruss
**Influential Woman, The: How to achieve success in your career – and still enjoy your personal life**   Lee Bryce
**Lure the Tiger Out of the Mountains: timeless tactics from the East for today's successful manager**   Gao Yuan
**Managing For Performance**   Alasdair White
**Managing Your Team**   John Spencer and Adrian Pruss
**Right Brain Time Manager, The**   Dr Harry Alder
**Seven Cultures of Capitalism, The: value systems for creating wealth in Britain, the United States, Germany, France, Japan, Sweden and the Netherlands**   Charles Hampden-Turner and Fons Trompenaars
**Smart Questions for Successful Managers**   Dorothy Leeds
**Think Like A Leader**   Dr Harry Alder

*Personnel and People Skills*

**Dealing with Difficult Colleagues**   Peter Wylie and Mardy Grothe
**Dealing with Difficult People**   Roberta Cava

**Psychological Testing for Managers**   Dr Stephanie Jones
**Reinventing Leadership**   Warren Bennis and Robert Townsend
**Tao of Negotiation: How to resolve conflict in all areas of your life**   Joel Edelman and Mary Beth Crain

*Financial Planning*

**Better Money Management**   Marie Jennings
**Financial Know-How for Non-Financial Managers**   John Spencer and Adrian Pruss
**How to Choose Stockmarket Winners**   Raymond Caley
**Perfectly Legal Tax Loopholes**   Stephen Courtney
**Practical Fundraising For Individuals And Small Groups**   David Wragg

*Small Businesses*

**How to Earn Money from Your Personal Computer**   Polly Bird
**How to Run a Part-Time Business**   Barrie Hawkins
**Making Money From Your Home**   Hazel Evans
**Marketing on a Tight Budget**   Patrick Forsyth
**Profit Through the Post: How to set up and run a successful mail order business**   Alison Cork

*Motivational*

**Play to Your Strengths**   Donald O. Clifton and Paula Nelson
**Super Success**   Philip Holden
**Winning Edge, The**   Charles Templeton

*Self-Improvement*

**Brain Power: the 12-week mental training programme**   Marilyn vos Savant and Leonore Fleischer
**Creative Thinking**   Michael LeBoeuf
**Napoleon Hill's Keys To Success**   Matthew Sartwell (ed.)
**Napoleon Hill's Unlimited Success**   Matthew Sartwell (ed.)
**Personal Growth Handbook, The**   Liz Hodgkinson
**Quantum Learning: unleash the genius within you**   Bobbi DePorter with Mike Hernacki
**Right Brain Manager, The: How to use the power of your mind to achieve personal and professional success**   Dr Harry Alder

**10-Minute Time And Stress Management**   Dr David Lewis
**Three Minute Meditator, The**   David Harp with Nina Feldman
**Total Confidence**   Philippa Davies

*Sales and Customer Services*

**Commonsense Marketing For Non-Marketers**   Alison Baverstock
**Creating Customers**   David H Bangs
**Enterprise One-to-One**   Don Peppers and Martha Rogers
**Guerrilla Marketing**   Jay Conrad Levinson
**Guerrilla Marketing Excellence**   Jay Conrad Levinson
**Guerrilla Marketing On The Internet**   Jay Conrad Levinson and
   Charles Rubin
**How to Succeed in Network Marketing**   Leonard Hawkins
**How to Win a Lot More Business in a Lot Less Time**   Michael
   LeBoeuf
**How to Win Customers and Keep Them for Life**   Michael LeBoeuf
**How to Write Letters that Sell**   Christian Godefroy and Dominique
   Glocheux
**Life's a Pitch: How to outwit your competitors and make a winning
   presentation**   Don Peppers
**One-to-One Future, The**   Don Peppers and Martha Rogers
**Professional Network Marketing**   John Bremner
**Sales Power: the Silva mind method for sales professionals**   Jose
   Silva and Ed Bernd Jr

*Presentation and Communication*

**Better Business Writing**   Maryann V. Piotrowski
**Confident Conversation**   Dr Lillian Glass
**Confident Speaking: how to communicate effectively using the
   Power Talk System**   Christian H Godefroy and Stephanie Barratt
**He Says, She Says: closing the communication gap between the
   sexes**   Dr Lillian Glass
**Powerspeak: the complete guide to public speaking and presentation**
   Dorothy Leeds
**Presenting Yourself: a personal image guide for men**   Mary Spillane
**Presenting Yourself: a personal image guide for women**   Mary
   Spillane
**Say What You Mean and Get What You Want**   George R. Walther
**Your Total Image**   Philippa Davies

*Careers and Training*

**How to Find the Perfect Job**   Tom Jackson
**Jobs for the Over 50s**   Linda Greenbury
**Making It as a Radio or TV Presenter**   Peter Baker
**Marketing Yourself: how to sell yourself and get the jobs you've always wanted**   Dorothy Leeds
**Networking and Mentoring: a woman's guide**   Dr Lily M. Segerman-Peck
**Perfect CV, The**   Tom Jackson
**Perfect Job Search Strategies**   Tom Jackson
**Secrets of Successful Interviews**   Dorothy Leeds
**Sharkproof: get the job you want, keep the job you love in today's tough job market**   Harvey Mackay
**10-Day MBA, The**   Steven Silbiger
**Which Way Now? – how to plan and develop a successful career**   Bridget Wright

For a free brochure with further information on our complete range of business titles, please write to:

**Piatkus Books**
**Freepost 7 (WD 4505)**
**London W1E 4EZ**

**PIATKUS**

## OTHER BOOKS BY DR HARRY ALDER

## NLP:
### The new art and science of getting what you want

This book places the concept of human excellence within everyone's reach. Learning the techniques of Neuro Linguistic Programming will produce dramatic benefits in many areas of your life, including selling and negotiating, creativity, public speaking, longterm memory, personal relationships, spelling and mental arithmetic, career advancement, listening and visual skills. By following Harry Alder's 21-day action plan, you too can uncover your hidden genius and develop your full potential for excellence.

## NLP For Managers:
### How to achieve excellence at work

NLP is changing the way managers communicate and perform. NLP enables you to understand and change how you think, feel and behave. It allows you to choose what to *do* in order to *have* or *be* what you want. The implications and benefits for the manager are enormous. You can use NLP to establish greater rapport with your clients, colleagues and staff, get your message across more clearly and persuasively, enjoy and excel in giving speeches and presentations, find new, creative ways to solve problems, reach the best decisions and much more.

## The Right Brain Manager
### How to harness the power of your mind to achieve personal and business success

The concept of the right brain - the intuitive, creative side as opposed to the logical, rational left side - has swept through the worlds of health, sports, creativity and learning. Now this new way of thinking is reaching the business person. In *The Right Brain Manager,* Dr Harry Alder describes how you can use your right brain to change the way you think about yourself, increase your skills and potential as a manager, and achieve greater success and effectiveness. The techniques revealed in this book are simple - and the results are extraordinary. Read *The Right Brain Manager* and uncover your full potential!

## The Right Brain Time Manager
**Practical new ways to maximise your time and revolutionise your life**

Here is a completely new and exciting way to make the most of your time and totally transform your life. In *The Right Brain Time Manager* you will learn how to use your subconscious to solve problems more quickly, prioritise your tasks effectively, use stress to increase your output and do more with your time, build in personal rewards to make you work faster and delegate and communicate effectively. By following this unique programme, you too can take control of your time and live your life to the full.

## Think Like A Leader
**150 top business leaders show you how their minds work**

*Think Like A Leader* brings together for the first time the thoughts and advice of 150 top business leaders and shows you how their minds work. By reading the book and following their successful thought patterns, you too can develop your leadership skills, learn how to generate brilliant ideas to give your business the edge, get ahead of your competitors and empower others to achieve their potential. Contributors include Robert Ayling, Managing Director of British Airways; Sir Nicholas Goodison, Chairman of TSB; and Sir Richard Greenbury, Chairman of Marks and Spencer.